The ALCHEMIST'S WAY

PAUL BOERGER

YOUR FREE GIFT

Thank you for purchasing *The Alchemist's Way*! As a token of my appreciation, I'm excited to offer you a special free gift.

I've created a *FREE* video training that provides a concise summary of the six core tenets of success, along with actionable steps you can take to implement them immediately.

To access this exclusive bonus content, visit www.thealchemistswaybook.com/bonus and register for your free materials.

This is my way of helping you kick-start your journey to unlocking your full potential and achieving amazing outcomes. Enjoy!

TABLE OF CONTENTS

PREFACE:
WHAT IS THE ALCHEMIST'S WAY?

Welcome, fellow traveler and future Alchemist. Before we embark on this journey, let me take a moment to acknowledge *you*—your experiences, your challenges, and your aspirations.

If you're here, it's because something within you is searching for more: more clarity, more confidence, more influence in the sometimes chaotic and unpredictable world of leadership.

I want you to know, you're not alone.

Leadership, especially in its raw and unpolished form, can feel like standing in the eye of a storm.

We've all been there, facing projects that feel insurmountable, deadlines that leave no breathing room, and team dynamics that sometimes seem to pull in every direction but the right one.

It's overwhelming, and yet, beneath that chaos lies potential waiting to be uncovered.

If you've ever felt the weight of those moments pressing on you, unsure of where to start or how to lead with confidence, know that I've walked that path, too. And this is where *The Alchemist's Way* finds its purpose.

At its core, it's about transformation—not just of your projects or your team but of you. It's a framework designed to empower leaders at any stage, taking you from uncertainty to mastery, helping you find your rhythm amidst the noise and discover your capacity to create something extraordinary.

Think of the modern-day Alchemist as a master of the philosopher's stone. It's about taking what feels disordered and turning it into something extraordinary—a true magnum opus of triumph!

Through a fusion of mystical leadership arts and scientific principles, this transformative process turns teams and individuals from molten crucibles of messy project workloads into cohesive, victorious forces.

The Alchemist's Way isn't just a method; it's a profound, metaphysical journey that helps you harness the power within, transmuting the ordinary into the extraordinary. It is anchored in the ingenious core tenets of leadership, where strategy meets intuition and even the most complex challenges are transformed into golden opportunities.

Join me, and let's embark on this epic adventure together. Along the way, we'll uncover the lessons, insights, and principles that make up the essence of *The Alchemist's Way*.

Together, we'll learn how to wield these leadership tools with the grace of an alchemical master. So, let's begin this journey and turn your leadership struggles into your greatest victories.

Sincerely,

The Alchemist, Your Alchemical Wizarding Warrior

PART I

THE MINDSET OF
THE ALCHEMIST

INTRO

This book isn't for the faint of heart.

It's for those who feel the pull of a bigger, brighter future and have the courage to reach for it.

Consider this a journey—one that might challenge you, inspire you, and perhaps make you question your sanity a time or two.

If I could promise an easy path, I would. But let's be real, growth isn't a leisurely stroll. It's more like a steep, rocky climb that might leave you a little scraped up.

As Alexis Carrel wisely put it, "A man cannot remake himself without suffering, for he is both the marble and the sculptor."

Yes, this journey may feel a little chisel-heavy, but that's where the magic happens.

To get the most out of this journey together, here's my first tip: relax. Let me explain.

If you want to grow your biceps, your muscle requires a great deal of physical stress and tension, followed by a period of rest. You repeat this process until the muscle achieves the desired growth.

The same is true for strengthening your legs, shoulders, lats, triceps, chest, back, etc. However, the brain is different.

Unlike any muscle in the human body, the brain paradoxically requires the exact opposite of tension for proper learning.

The brain must be relaxed for it to learn, develop, and grow.

For you to get the most from these pages, I recommend this five-step process:

- **Relax:** Find a comfortable spot, and get into a peaceful state.
- **Read:** Engage with each idea.
- Visualize: Picture yourself living these principles.
- **Reflect:** Take time to let it all sink in.

- **Act:** The book without action defeats my purpose for writing it.

The journey ahead is about becoming the best version of yourself, growing, giving, and embracing those closest to you as you reach for your worthy goals and ultimately, life's best.

If you're still reading, let me make a promise: there is gold here. Pure, hard-earned, life-changing gold.

But here's the truth—most people won't make it to the finish line. So, the question is: are you in, or have I lost you already?

If you're in and ready to take on a challenge and reach a goal that could change your life, then let's go.

Life's not easy, and finding mentors to guide you? Even harder. But if you've got a dream that's been tugging at you, one that might have slipped through your fingers a time or two, then this book might be exactly what you need.

Hold onto that dream of yours, because we're about to light up your path. Welcome to *The Alchemist's Way*—a journey that just might turn your world into gold.

CHAPTER 1: MISMATCHED BOOKENDS

On May 10, 2024, I found myself in a whirlwind of emotions: laughter, tears, and profound introspection, as I attended my daughter Alexa's college graduation.

In this nostalgic moment, I was thinking that this is a thirty-seven-year journey, split into two defining events—like mismatched bookends framing a dramatic stage play—that handed me not one, but two beginnings.

This is the story of the *Tale of Two Degrees*—a journey that transformed me from a fresh-faced engineer, eager to "change the world," to a grizzled single dad with more gray hair than I'd bargained for and enough dad jokes to launch a comedy tour.

From the back of the auditorium, I witnessed a sea of friends and family, all gathered to celebrate this incredible class of graduates. We waited with anxious anticipation for her name to be called.

To this day, that moment is indelibly etched in my memory—watching her confidently stride across the stage to receive her diploma from the dean of engineering.

"Today is my daughter's graduation day," I murmured to myself, trying to swallow the painful lump in my throat and calm the pounding in my chest. It was nearly impossible to hold back the tears of love and inspiration.

Like mine, her journey had been fraught with challenges and determination, making this day even more special.

As she exited the stage, she was greeted with a gauntlet of enthusiastic high-fives from the faculty and staff—a sight that finally broke through my tear ducts, releasing some of the biggest emotions I've ever felt.

After returning to their seats, the master of ceremonies shared a few words that made my heart swell even more.

When the graduating class of 2024 shifted their tassels from right to left—the timeless ritual that signifies transition—my eyes welled up, and my breath caught in my throat. It was a defining moment; my little girl had grown into a remarkable woman, ready to conquer the world.

I found myself swept up in a whirlwind of laughter, tears, pride, and nostalgia.

I've raised her as a single dad since she was five years old, and our journey was one of challenge, hope, and mutual healing. To see her cross that stage was to see a future brimming with possibility, all born from a love that carried us through countless sleepless late-night conversations, science projects, and heart-to-heart talks.

As I reflected on Alexa's achievement, I couldn't help but draw parallels to my own journey.

Earlier that morning, as I dressed for the ceremony, memories came flooding back. Exactly thirty-seven years earlier, on May 10, 1987, I stood on a similar stage, awkwardly posing for photos with my parents, clutching my freshly minted Bachelor of Science in Electrical Engineering.

Little did I know that life would take me on a roller coaster ride of unexpected twists and turns, finally bringing me to this fateful day.

Over those thirty-seven years, I evolved from a new graduate to an engineer, leader, manager, and most importantly, a father. Alexa was my miracle, bringing true meaning into my life.

As a single dad, I had the privilege of raising this beautiful, kind-hearted soul, and this day marked her entry into the fascinating world of engineering.

My beautiful Alexa chose to carry the torch of engineering in a new direction, pursuing her Bachelor of Science in Mechanical and Aerospace Engineering with a focus on space travel.

Curiosity, innovation, and hard work had formed a generational legacy, bound by these two events. Yet, I couldn't help but introspect on the vast chasm between our journeys.

Between the Bookends

As I ponder those mismatched bookends spanning 37 years, I can't help but wish someone had handed me a roadmap back then—a guide to navigate the challenges, missteps, and triumphs that lay ahead.

At the tender age of twenty-two, I was brimming with eagerness, yet I wandered through the unknown, desperate for the guidance I lacked.

If I could send a message to my younger self across time, it would carry the distilled wisdom of experience—the lessons I now hold dear. These truths would have been a compass, accelerating my growth, maturity, accomplishments, and path to confidence while sparing me countless detours of heartache and self-doubt.

Today, I offer these lessons to you, not just as a reflection of my journey, but as a beacon for yours. May they light the path ahead, guiding you through moments of struggle, inspiring resilience, and fueling your pursuit of purpose.

This is where our story truly begins—a story of legacy, resilience, and the passing of the torch from one generation to the next.

Because what we build isn't just for today—it's for the future, for those who will follow, and for the dreams yet to be realized.

Key Points

- **The Power of Legacy:** Passing on knowledge and passion to the next generation is one of life's greatest rewards.

- **Perseverance Through Challenges:** The journey may be tough, but each step, no matter how difficult, leads to growth and new opportunities.

- **The Joy of Seeing Others Succeed:** Watching our loved ones chase their dreams and succeed is far more fulfilling than any personal accomplishment.

- **The Importance of Adaptability:** Life doesn't follow a perfect script. Embrace the unexpected twists, and you'll discover new strengths and passions along the way.

CHAPTER 2:
THE NASCENT ALCHEMIST

For most of my life, money was a scarce commodity. You guessed it. We didn't have it.

For this reason, I've had a job since the age of twelve. These were NOT glamorous jobs, and all were VERY physical. Although they didn't have cachet, they nurtured a great work ethic—even stronger than the calluses on my hands.

The Nascent Alchemist: My Journey from Small-Town Dreamer to an Alchemist

Growing up in the rural Midwest, our economy was pretty weak and didn't offer a lot of options for the average youth, but I was able to find work—nothing glamorous, just a string of very physical, very humbling roles that taught me a thing or two about hard work and earning my own way.

By high school, I was working six days a week while my peers were busy living their best teenage lives—joining sports teams, pushing curfews, or perfecting the fine art of doing absolutely nothing.

My time was spent clocking hours, driven by necessity, but also by something deeper. Growing up in a small Midwestern town like Marshalltown, Iowa, a place more famous for its pigs than its people, didn't exactly offer a clear path to big dreams.

Yet, even as I punched the clock and trudged through my daily grind, something quietly took root within me: a yearning to create something bigger than myself.

It wasn't just about survival or chasing a paycheck. Somewhere in the depths of my soul, I wanted my life's work to *matter*—to extend beyond the borders of my small town, beyond my own needs, and into something that could impact others.

It was an unspoken desire to leave a mark, to build something that would stand the test of time, and to find meaning in a world that often felt like a sea of routine.

Engineering Dreams and REO Speedwagon Visions

As I stumbled into adulthood, I navigated the treacherous waters of engineering school, financing my education with a patchwork of student loans and lots of hours in minimum-wage jobs.

Let's just say I had no idea what I was doing, but I was stubborn enough to keep going.

My only real dream? Inspired by REO Speedwagon's "Riding the Storm Out," I had this vision of living in a tiny A-frame cabin on a small mountain lake in Colorado and enduring a Rocky Mountain snowstorm while listening to REO tunes. Not exactly the loftiest of dreams, but it was mine.

And somehow, I made it. I graduated from college—financially bankrupt, emotionally lacking, and with no relevant experience or clear plan for success.

My only assets? A strong work ethic, a freshly minted engineering degree, and the ability to hold my beer like an Olympic champion. The odds were not exactly in my favor as I entered the competitive workforce in high tech, but at least I had a vision to chase.

From $60 to a Passion for Technology

With only $60 to my name, I moved to Colorado, determined to make that REO Speedwagon vision a reality.

Within three weeks, I landed my first professional job as an electrical engineer at Apogee Robotics, a penny stock company with big dreams and fun technology spaces. Robots are way cool to a geek like me.

Suddenly, I found myself immersed in a world of autonomous propulsion systems, blinking lights, buzzers, automation, and all things electromechanical.

It was my perfect playground.

It was at Apogee that my interest in technology leadership took root. I discovered a passion for design, hardware, firmware, software, project management, and all things geeky.

The thrill of designing, building, and collaborating wasn't just about solving problems; it was about connecting with others to craft something meaningful together.

That's when I knew: I didn't just want to succeed for myself. I wanted to inspire, to lead, and to shape a future where my efforts could ripple outward, affecting more lives than I could ever imagine.

It was a great and fun start to my career.

Thirty-Seven Years of Engineering Adventures

Now, thirty-seven years later, I've led engineering teams and delivered over 100 innovations in products and services to the market.

Today, I share those lessons of leadership with tomorrow's leaders via *The Alchemist's Way*.

For me, the journey was nothing short of miraculous, filled with unexpected twists, setbacks, and the occasional moment of divine intervention.

Reflecting on those early career years, I was woefully unprepared. I had no mentors, no money, and not even a glimmer of what success looked like.

To make things more challenging, my family (God bless them) never quite saw me as anything other than the youngest sibling of four and a perpetual goofball. Did that limiting belief affect my journey? You bet it did. But what they lacked in belief, they made up for in love.

And sometimes, that's all you need.

The Transformation Through Work Ethic, Belief, and Vision

Feeling unsure of the journey ahead, I found solace in a killer work ethic, good health, and a loosely forming vision of the leader I aspired to be.

Over time, something incredible began to happen; my confidence grew, not from having all the answers, but from trusting the process.

I learned to have faith in the unknown, and that belief became a catalyst. It propelled me forward, driving me to develop the skills, adopt the behaviors, and cultivate the expertise critical for success.

It wasn't just about gathering technical knowledge; it was about mastering the craft of leadership itself, understanding people, solving problems, and seeing the big picture with clarity. Each step transformed me, building a foundation that turned uncertainty into strength and potential into achievement.

Looking back, my story isn't one of personal triumph; it's a testament to the transformative power of determination, belief, and an unwavering vision.

The Bible says, "Now faith is the substance of things hoped for, the evidence of things not seen." For me, faith provided the preview of the life I wanted, even when the path ahead was dark and full of unknowns.

Every challenge, every setback, and every lack of resources was just a stepping stone on the path to success.

I'm immensely grateful for the journey because it has shaped me in profoundly beautiful ways, even if it did leave me with a few more gray hairs and wrinkles than I'd planned.

Lessons from the Road Less Traveled

The road wasn't easy. It was filled with hazards, obstacles, successes, failures, and too many betrayals to count.

When it comes to betrayals, I have a lot of scars, and not even one of them is from an enemy. They are all people that I trusted and loved.

Betrayal is tough because it is loss wrapped in pain that can make one lose our greatest gift—hope. But when hope returns, it brings with it an awesome seed of resilience, and I am convinced that resilience can only be taught through failure and perhaps betrayal.

So, here's to the journey—the stumbles, the triumphs, and everything in between. Because in the end, the struggle to become who you're meant to be is what makes life truly worthwhile.

Key Points

- **Faith and Vision Are Essential:** Even when the path ahead is unclear, having faith in your vision can be the light that guides you.
- **A Strong Work Ethic Beats a Lack of Resources:** I may have lacked everything else, but a solid work ethic kept me moving forward. No matter how tough things got, I knew that I could count on it.

- **Resilience Grows from Adversity:** Every setback, failure, and betrayal taught me resilience. And it's this resilience that turns ordinary people into extraordinary leaders.
- **Belief in Yourself Is the Ultimate Catalyst:** Your belief in yourself will drive you to learn, grow, and succeed, even when no one else seems to believe in you.

CHAPTER 3: WHY TEACH LEADERSHIP? BECAUSE WE ARE ALL LEADERS!

L et me say that again, just in case you missed it: We. Are. All. Leaders.

- Have you ever wanted to make the world a better place?
- Have you ever hoped to see your kids succeed (without having to bribe them with snacks)?
- Have you ever wished to make an impact in your neighborhood or community? Maybe you dreamed of leaving your mark on the universe, even if it's just a tiny dent?

Guess what? At some point, we all have. And that's the unmistakable call of leadership—the call that we're all meant to answer.

But before you go running off to change the world, there's one important thing to know: leadership starts with you.

The very first call of leadership is self-mastery. Before we can lead others, we have to lead ourselves, because if you can't get yourself organized, how do you expect to inspire a team to follow you?

The Accidental Leader

As mentioned, I've had a job since I was twelve years old. If I wanted clothes, haircuts, lunch tickets, a car, gas money, an education, or just some pocket change, my life demanded that I work for it. That early introduction to responsibility was like a crash course in life skills.

I call myself an "accidental leader" because, in my late teens, leadership found me, whether I was ready or not.

Whenever there was a job to be done, I'd often find myself being appointed as the team leader, supervisor, or manager. And almost every time, I was both honored and a little surprised. ("Wait, you want me in charge? Are you sure about that?")

Why Teach Leadership?

Leadership is a powerful force that impacts every area of our lives. It's not just about managing teams or running companies; it's about guiding families, supporting communities, and championing causes. It's about being the person others can rely on, whether it's at work, at home, or anywhere in between.

And the best part? You don't have to be a CEO or a tech guru to be a leader.

Leaders come in all shapes and sizes.

You might be leading your family, guiding a team, advocating for a cause, or simply leading yourself to a better life.

We are ALL called to lead at various stages of our lives, and every time we answer that call, we grow.

The Groovy Journey of Leadership

Leadership isn't just about making decisions or calling the shots; it's a soulful, spiritual journey where you get to make a genuine impact on the lives you touch. It demands more from you than you can anticipate, shaping your identity into the ultimate expression of your values, character, abilities, heart, and purpose.

It's an awesome journey for those who seek to excel—think of it as a road trip where the destination is personal mastery, and the playlist is nothing but the greatest hits.

But let's not kid ourselves—stepping into leadership takes courage. It means facing headwinds of scrutiny, exposing your weaknesses, and embracing vulnerability. It's about standing firm in your convictions, weathering setbacks, and handling criticism with grace (and maybe just a touch of humor).

Join me on this odyssey of life leadership, stepping into the footprints of the Leadership Alchemist—a figure infused with fiery passion for creation, attainment, and a heart to serve.

True leaders don't just lead; they inspire.

They stand their ground, forgive, and keep pushing forward.

An Odyssey of Life Leadership

I've often said, "If you don't need change, you don't need a leader." The same applies to your life situation. If you are dissatisfied with where you are in life, it's time to take charge and lead yourself to a new destination.

- If you want to change your life, lead it!
- If you want to change your results, lead it!
- If you want to change your future, lead it!
- If you want to change your outcomes, lead it!
- If you want to change your corner of the world, lead it!

You've got it in you to go the distance, so become one of the few, the difference-makers, the ones who spot greatness in others and guide them to their full potential.

Personal mastery creates the foundation and pathway to step into the circle of game-changers, where your journey becomes a legacy of positive influence, attainment, and transformative impact.

So, I challenge you to take that step into the club of difference-makers and world-changers. Because once you do, you won't just be leading—you'll be creating a ripple effect that touches everyone around you.

Take the Leap!

I won't sugarcoat it, leadership isn't easy.

Leadership is a great privilege and an enormous responsibility, but it's also the greatest journey you'll ever take.

As a leader, others are looking to you, counting on you, because YOU are the one to help them become the best version of themselves.

As a leader, others will look to you, count on you, and some will trust you to help them step into the fullest expression of their gifts. Together, you'll pursue shared success and achieve what once seemed impossible.

Take the leap. Join the ranks of those who dare to lead, those who dare to make a difference. I promise—it will be worth it.

Key Points

- **We Are All Leaders:** Leadership isn't limited to CEOs or high-profile figures; it's a role we all play at different stages of our lives, whether in our families, communities, or careers.

- **Leadership Begins with Self-Mastery:** Before leading others, you need to lead yourself. Self-discipline, self-awareness, and personal growth are the first steps on this journey.

- **Leadership Requires Courage and Vulnerability:** True leadership involves standing firm in your convictions, handling scrutiny with grace, and embracing vulnerability to inspire others. It's truly a dance!

- **The Journey Is Worth It**: Becoming a leader is about creating a legacy of positive influence. It's a challenging but deeply fulfilling journey that allows you to help others reach their potential.

CHAPTER 4: ENTER THE ALCHEMIST—THE SAGE OF LEADERSHIP

*I*n the ancient art of alchemy, lead was transmuted into gold through a delicate fusion of elements and mastery over the crucible. The alchemist's patience was unmatched—metals were slowly heated in the crucible for years, shedding their original nature to evolve into their highest form.

Some say this process of alchemy purified not just the metals, but the soul itself.

The Alchemist's Way is a soulful journey toward becoming the best version of ourselves, a quest for self-mastery, growth, and purpose.

Why should we strive for our highest form? Because the journey of self-improvement is the most purposeful and meaningful pursuit we can undertake. It's a groovy, fulfilling ride that makes life worth living.

The Quest for Your Best Self

How do you become the best version of yourself? It starts by identifying your strengths, embracing your passions, and taking a hard look at what makes you come alive.

When you're inspired by a great purpose, an extraordinary project, or a compelling goal, you break free from your limitations.

As Patanjali, the ancient sage, once said, "Dormant forces, faculties, and talents become alive, and you discover yourself to be a greater person by far than you ever dreamed." Let's empower those dormant forces, faculties, and talents to come alive and find our passion!

Without passion, you can't fuel your journey of becoming the best version of yourself.

The best leaders, athletes, parents, and teachers share this trait—they all have a passion for their craft.

Without excitement and drive, the road to growth and achievement becomes a slog rather than a soulful journey.

The Journey Is Yours Alone

Through the following pages, I want you to focus on *your* journey, not someone else's.

Don't try to emulate someone else's success, live their dreams, or chase their goals.

This is your path, and it begins and ends with you. You are the champion of your own life, the one who must chart the course to becoming the best version of yourself.

There is no greater expression of who you are than reaching your full potential.

To strive to be your best self is to engage in a never-ending process of growth and achievement, like a seed growing into a magnificent flower.

The Seed That Becomes a Flower

Picture a seed planted deep in the dark soil. It doesn't settle for being just a seed; it instinctively reaches for the light, striving for its highest form.

Slowly, it transforms, breaking through the soil as a seedling, stretching upward as a thriving plant, and finally blossoming into a breathtaking flower.

Now, ask yourself: Have you bloomed into your best self, or are you still a seedling, waiting for the right moment to grow?

A Calling to Bloom

Like that seed, every one of us carries an innate calling to grow, evolve, and become the fullest expression of our potential.

But the journey doesn't stop at blooming. Once we've reached our peak, we share the bounty of our talents and gifts with the world around us.

A flower doesn't bloom for itself; it contributes beauty, sustenance, and inspiration to its environment.

The process of surpassing yourself isn't about perfection—it's about progress. It's about embracing the challenges and transformations that help you grow into the person you were meant to be.

So, plant your roots, reach for the light, and commit to blooming into your most magnificent self. The world is waiting for your full expression.

The Wisdom of Queen Christina

Queen Christina of Sweden once said, "It is necessary to try to surpass oneself always; this occupation ought to last as long as life." She wasn't kidding. She knew that true success lies in continuous growth and self-improvement.

Life is about surpassing yourself, growing beyond your current limits, and seeking new heights.

Growth: The Heart of Our Journey

Life is growth. As the saying goes, "When you're green, you're growing; when you're ripe, you rot."

We're all on a journey of constant growth, cycling through goal setting and achievement.

With each cycle comes new skills, insights, and fulfillment. Life can only be navigated successfully through this incremental art of attainment.

Lessons from the Alchemist

The Alchemist's journey is all about growth, discovery, and the pursuit of excellence.

Through the art of self-leadership and mastery, you can turn your ordinary life into something extraordinary. Whether it's leading a team, nurturing your family, or championing a cause, you must first lead yourself.

The Alchemist's Way transforms challenges into gold—be it for teams, families, churches, or communities. It will arm and weaponize future alchemists to become all that they are capable of becoming—the best versions of themselves.

The Six Core Tenets of Leadership Alchemy

To master this art, the Leadership Alchemist focuses on six core tenets:

- **The 3 C's of Goal Setting (Clear, Concise, and Compelling):** Goals are the blueprint. The Leadership Alchemist crafts them meticulously, ensuring they're clear, concise, and irresistibly compelling.

- **Building Belief:** Just as an alchemist believes in transformation, the leader instills unwavering belief in themselves and their team, turning doubt into determination.

- **Character and Integrity:** Character is the crucible's purity. Integrity forms the bedrock of leadership, building trust and strength over time.

- **Vitality and Energy:** Like the alchemist harnesses vital forces, a leader brings energy and enthusiasm, energizing the team and amplifying their collective power.

- **Daily Habits and Morning Rituals:** Consistency is key. The Leadership Alchemist creates daily habits that set the tone for success, just as rituals are vital in alchemy.

- **The Heart of Servant Leadership:** The heart guides the process. A servant leader knows that every triumph is a collaborative effort, and true success comes from serving others.

From Chaos to Success

In the alchemical journey of leadership, chaos becomes the crucible of creation, and misguided paths lead to purposeful outcomes.

The Alchemist turns the base elements of life—problems, opportunities, families, teams, communities—into the gold of success, harmony, and fulfillment.

Through a blend of intention, perseverance, and belief, even the toughest challenges can be transformed into triumphs.

The Path Forward

So, how do you take an ordinary life and turn it into something extraordinary? It starts with a commitment to continuous growth, a willingness to face adversity, persistence, and a passion for finding your purpose.

Through these pages, *The Alchemist's Way* shall serve as your guide on how to transmute your challenges into opportunities, set clear goals, build belief, and lead with character and heart.

Together, we'll walk the path of the Alchemist, turning your aspirations into a legacy of success.

If you're ready to turn your lead into gold, keep reading. Your transformation awaits.

Key Points

- **Leadership Begins with Self-Mastery:** Before you can lead others, you must lead yourself by finding your passions, strengths, and purpose.

- **Growth Is a Lifelong Journey:** Continuous self-improvement and surpassing your current limits are at the core of personal and professional success.

- **The Six Core Tenets of The Alchemist's Way:** Focus on clear goals, strong belief, character, vitality, consistent habits, and a servant's heart to transform challenges into success.

- **Transformation Through Intention and Passion:** The Leadership Alchemist teaches how to turn the ordinary into the extraordinary by infusing life with purpose, growth, and resilience.

CHAPTER 5: THE ALCHEMIST'S MENTAL GUIDE— MATURITY, LEADERSHIP, & MINDSET

On my first meetings with mentees and aspiring managers, I like to start with stories of my early career struggles—the kind of missteps that make you cringe, but also laugh a little. (I mean, who hasn't accidentally CC'd the wrong "Bob" on an email and set off a chain reaction?)

One of the biggest challenges I share is my journey to professional maturity. And no, it's not about knowing when to finally buy a proper cell phone or briefcase—it's about mastering the balance between courage and consideration.

Professional Maturity: Finding the Balance

So, what is professional maturity? Simply put, it's the art of balancing courage and consideration.

Think of it like a seesaw—too much courage, and you're bulldozing your team; too much consideration, and you're getting bulldozed.

The sweet spot of courage and consideration? That's where the magic happens, and where effective leadership lives.

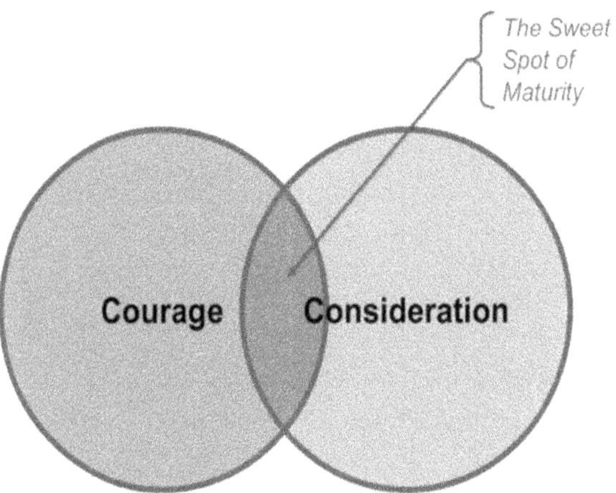

The key is striking that balance and dancing in the sweet spot of maturity.

I like to illustrate this balance with a simple Venn diagram: two circles, one labeled "Courage" and the other "Consideration," overlapping to form a beautiful, harmonious middle. That middle is what we aim for—steady, balanced, and capable of taking bold actions without trampling on anyone's toes (or egos).

To help aspiring leaders find that balance, I share two key insights in the balance of this chapter:

- **For courage,** master the art of going first.
- **For consideration,** master the art of going last.

The Leadership Dimension

But here's where things get even more interesting.

When I mentor new managers, I introduce a second Venn diagram. This one isn't just about the balance of courage and consideration—it adds a third circle: Team Focus. And this is where the true "Leadership Mindshift" happens.

Team focus is about shifting from a "me focus" to a "we focus." It's understanding that leadership isn't just about your individual performance; it's about the collective success of your team.

Imagine three overlapping circles: Courage, Consideration, and Team Focus. Right in the middle, where all three intersect, is what I call "Professional Maturity 2.0"—or as I like to think of it, the point where you've officially graduated from being just a manager to becoming a true leader.

As with my journey, aspiring leaders often struggle with this shift because it requires letting go of the need to control every little thing. Instead, you're empowering others to succeed, even if that means stepping back and letting them make (and learn from) their own mistakes.

It's a bit like teaching a teenager to drive— nerve-wracking at first, but essential for their growth (and perhaps at the expense of my hairline).

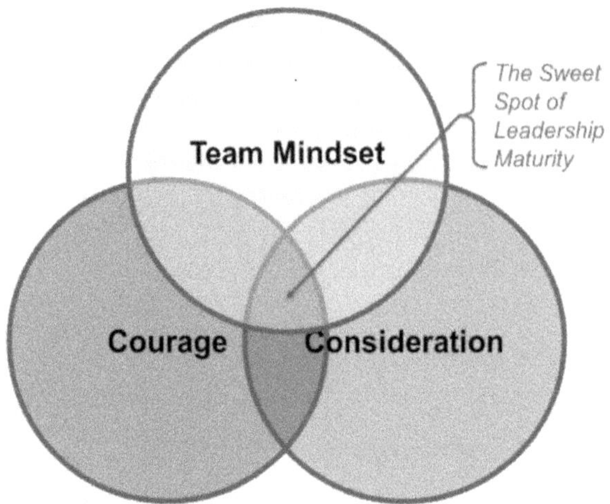

These mindsets are the foundation of the Alchemist's toolkit, shaping the essence of professional maturity.

So, how do we start this journey toward maturity? We begin with courage—the courage to go first, to lead by example, and to show vulnerability. It's the first and most crucial step, because without it, the rest of the balancing act doesn't stand a chance.

Mastering the Art of "Going First"

Mastering courage is about making the tough calls, asking the uncomfortable questions, and pushing yourself (and your team) out of your comfort zones. It's about acknowledging that sometimes you'll stumble, but that's okay. After all, nobody became a master alchemist overnight.

Courage doesn't mean charging into a meeting with all guns blazing, declaring your opinions as if they're gospel. Well, not exactly.

Courage, in leadership, is about taking the first step—whether that's voicing a difficult truth, admitting a mistake, or setting a new direction. It's about embracing vulnerability and showing your team that it's okay to be a little uncomfortable if it means moving forward.

When I encourage young managers to master the art of going first, I remind them that courage is contagious.

If you're willing to step up and lead by example, your team will follow. It's like being the first one to dance at a wedding—awkward at first, but suddenly everyone's on the floor, grooving along. (Bonus points if you can do it without stepping on anyone's toes.)

Here's an example I use to drive the point home: Have you ever walked into a party where everyone is already engaged, laughing, and talking in tight little groups, leaving you standing there, clutching your drink like a lifeline? Yep, welcome to adulthood. And welcome to one of the first challenges of leadership: taking initiative.

As a tall, awkward, shy kid growing up in the Midwest, I often found myself the target of ridicule, and with that came a lot of insecurities, which especially manifested in organized social situations.

How bad was my shyness? For the first decades of my life, I was terrified of popcorn introductions.

Shortly after moving to Colorado, our apartment complex hosted a meet-and-greet gathering for its residents at the clubhouse.

I walked in, and everyone seemed to know each other, so I remember standing there awkwardly alone before finally wandering over to the bar to grab a drink, where I had high hopes of talking to a friendly bartender.

As I approached the bottom of the glass, I began eyeing a path across the crowded room to plan my exit.

To my surprise, an older gentleman came up to me, offering a friendly handshake and introducing himself with a compliment on my firm handshake. He then introduced me to his lovely wife, and we engaged in conversation.

Whew. All at once, I felt the anxiety melt and leave my body with a deep exhale. It was at that moment that I knew I was going to have to beat my fears and be more like that friendly guy and his wife. They were fantastic, and they showed me how to be courageous with a first extended hand of friendship.

When the student is ready, the teacher shall appear. There was an aha moment when I realized that the world is full of shy people in gatherings just waiting for someone to give them a smile and a friendly hello.

Overcoming my introversion was one of my first battles in leadership, and it pushed me to step out of my comfort zone and make those awkward-but-necessary first introductions.

Throughout my career, I've led projects and teams of engineers that I affectionately call the "herd of nerds." I can't make fun of them, because they are my peeps, and I AM one.

One lesson stands out that carried me deep into my leadership journey: the importance of going first.

Taking that first step, venturing into unknown territory, and breaking the ice—whether in a meeting, a project, or a conversation—it's a quintessential skill every leader must master.

Because here's the thing: the team is counting on you to bring it!

Leading isn't about following a well-worn path; it often means charting new territories, navigating uncharted waters, and looking like a fool as you stumble through the dark.

That awkwardness of going first is what sets exceptional leaders apart.

When teammates see you take that courageous leap, they think, "Hey, this might be a safe space to take risks." And that's where the magic begins.

Key Points

- **Embrace the Discomfort:** The discomfort of going first is a small price to pay for the transformative power it brings to leadership.

- **Be the Pioneer:** Being a pioneer is not about being fearless; it's about embracing fear and stepping forward anyway.

Challenge

As mentioned, when I mentor aspiring leaders, I share the story of mastering the art of going first, and then I give them the following challenge to drive the lesson home.

• Challenge: Many are afraid of failure, but if you're with me, this week, I want you to flex that muscle of courage and put yourself out there. Meet five new people and share your experience with me. It will open unexpected doors.

Mastering the Art of "Going Last"

If you ever find yourself in a position of influence within any relationship, here's a golden rule: Go last.

I know it might sound a tad counterintuitive to the prior message of championing the act of going first, but trust me, this point is crucial.

When you master the art of going first, you flex that muscle of courage, but now let's look at the yin to that yang.

Courage alone cannot navigate the intricate web of human relationships.

Consideration emerges as the silent force, binding us in empathy and understanding.

Consideration means knowing when to step back and let others take the lead. This is the art of going last—listening, observing, and valuing everyone's input before deciding.

It's the polar opposite of hogging the spotlight—it allows others to shine!

Going last doesn't mean you're hesitant or passive; it means you're giving space for others to contribute.

You're building trust, encouraging collaboration, and showing that every voice matters.

It's like letting everyone else order first at a restaurant—you're making sure nobody feels rushed.

It's the art of stepping back, listening intently, and allowing others to bask in the limelight. Going last communicates a profound sense of care and respect, nurturing connections that transcend the superficial.

In the complexity of relationships, consideration lays the foundation for trust, empathy, and mutual respect to flourish.

Why master the art of going last? It communicates how much we truly care. It's about consideration. To illustrate this in action, consider the following situations:

- **Hosting a Dinner Party:** Feed everyone before going through the buffet line. Be the gracious host who ensures everyone is taken care of before tending to your own plate—go last.

- **Welcoming Your Partner**: When you see your partner, find out how their day went before sharing your own experiences. It's a small act that says,

"Your feelings and experiences matter to me"—go last.

- **Connecting with Your Kids:** When your kids come home from school, take the time to learn about their day before launching into tales of your own. It shows them that their world is important to you—go last.

- **In a Working Session:** During a team meeting, hear everyone's opinions before sharing your own thoughts. It not only fosters a collaborative environment but also demonstrates respect for diverse perspectives—go last.

Remember, people don't care about what you know until they know that you care. This is where the true essence of leadership comes into play. And in the grand tapestry of relationships, holding the door for others becomes a symbolic gesture—a small act that cements connections and showcases the art of going last.

So be the one who helps loved ones put on their jacket, be the last to sit at the table, hold that door for others, and be the last to speak in a working session.

When we put together the messages of going first and going last, we arrive at maturity—a delicate balance of courage and consideration.

Key Points

- **It's Not About Speed:** When it comes to consideration, reduce the need for efficiency and reduce the tempo. Going last isn't about being the slowest; it's about being the most considerate.

- **It's a Dance:** The art of going last is a dance of empathy and understanding that requires time. Don't rush it. Picture a candlelit evening with your greatest romance tunes playing in the background. These are the softened moments that lead to our harmonious relationships.

- **Amplify Your Impact:** In a world that often rushes to be heard, going last ensures your voice is heard in the hearts of those you lead. What acts of consideration are most important to you? Hear your answer and respond in kind.

Challenge

As mentioned, when I mentor aspiring leaders, I share the story of mastering the art of going last, and then I give them the following challenge to drive the lesson home.

• Challenge: This week, I want you to flex that muscle of consideration and consciously put others' needs before yours. At work and at home, practice the art of going last. Even though it can become difficult and you may struggle, at the end, commit to doing this today and share your experience with me.

Leadership Mindshift: Adding a Third Dimension

Transitioning from individual contributor to leader demands a seismic shift in priorities. It beckons us to relinquish the attraction of personal excellence and embrace the collective vision of the team.

Forging ahead with unwavering focus, we learn to harness the strengths of our team, steering toward shared objectives and team victories.

It's a journey of self-discovery and transformation, where personal success intertwines with the triumphs of the collective.

As we embark on this odyssey, let us embrace the delicate balance between courage, consideration, and team focus. Let us unravel the mysteries of leadership with humility and grace, forging bonds that withstand the test of time. Together, we navigate the complexities of human interaction, weaving a tapestry of trust, camaraderie, and shared purpose.

Why did you get promoted to leadership? Like many of us, it's because you were REALLY good at your job.

- You were present.
- You took ownership.
- You showed up.
- You showcased your gifts and talents.
- You demonstrated commitment.
- You shined among your peers.
- Your outcomes were consistently great.

So, when the business need allows, you get the promotion... and... voila, you're a leader!

So now what?

You were promoted because you were good at your job, but completely unaware of the leadership skills necessary to be successful.

This new role didn't come with an instruction manual.

Early successful entrepreneurs often find themselves in a similar situation, where they must hire a team to help with the workload. As soon as you begin hiring staff, you're in a position of leadership—whether you want it or not.

Earlier this week, one entrepreneur asked, "What advice would you give to an entrepreneur just starting their first business and needing a team?"

My answer: "Learn leadership—quickly!"

These early-career managers are categorically the *"accidental leaders."*

What is an accidental leader? This person didn't set out to lead, but because they were good at their job, they found themselves getting promoted, getting more responsibility, getting direct reports—until they're officially anointed team lead or manager.

These are the accidental leaders. They are given responsibility, but often not support.

As for my leadership journey, one of the hardest shifts in leadership was to shift from personal excellence and performance to an acute focus on speed, quality, and success of those around me. It stemmed from seeing those around me succeed.

To truly lead, I had to let go of personal performance goals and dive headfirst into team focus.

Stepping into the Unknown

As mentioned, when I was in my late teens, leadership roles started coming my way (competition wasn't too stiff. LOL).

When I was in my early twenties, the leadership calling beckoned once again. I had several successful projects under my belt. My portfolio had grown into something of significance.

However, in the technology arena, the expectations of leadership were much more demanding than a résumé full of accomplishments. Most didn't care about achievements, domain knowledge, or the need for rapid results—they had much bigger needs.

They desperately wanted to succeed. They wanted to see their fingerprints on a great project and have confidence in a guide who could get them to where they wanted to go.

To remain in a leadership role, my calling required that I get better—a LOT better. Ready or not, I had to begin a new journey, as I had become the accidental leader.

Some aspects of leadership, I did well; others, not so much. I found that I was connecting with like-minded individuals who were focused on speed and rapid results.

However, I struggled with influencing the introverts, slower talkers, and the detail-oriented staffers who moved a little slower. These talented engineers were getting left behind—and miserable—under my influence.

As the bar was raised, I was quickly learning the benefit of utilizing the carrot over the stick.

I often reflect on the words of John Wooden, "If you want to go fast, go alone. If you want to go far, you need a team."

This is where the greatest shift occurs. It's that aha moment when every leader realizes that everything we do is with and through others.

Let me repeat this important point: As a leader, everything we do is with and through others.

In the hustle and bustle of business, it's easy to get caught up in personal achievements and individual glory. But true leadership isn't about standing in the spotlight alone; it's about shining that light on your team and empowering them to succeed.

As leaders, we must shift our mindset from self-promotion to team effectiveness.

It's about fostering an environment where everyone feels valued, heard, and motivated to contribute their best.

Some of the keys to bringing out the best in others...

- See the best in others
- Showcase their strengths

- Don't compete with the team
- Don't judge the team
- Give the team your very best
- Serve them well and be their champion and ambassador!

When we prioritize our team's success over our personal accolades, magic happens.

We build stronger bonds, foster greater innovation, and achieve remarkable results together.

After all, everyone loves to be on a winning team!

So, to all the leaders out there… remember, your team is your greatest asset. Invest in them, support them, and celebrate their successes as your own.

Because in the end, it's not about what you achieve alone; it's about what you accomplish together.

Key Points

- **Maturity:** Professional maturity = balancing courage and consideration. Tip the scale too far, and you're either a bulldozer or a doormat. Neither is ideal.

- **Lessons of Going First and Last:** Master the art of going first (courage) and going last (consideration). Your team will thank you, even if they don't say it out loud.

- **3D of Team Focus:** Add team focus, and you're officially playing three-dimensional leadership chess. It's not about you; it's about us.

- **Don't Seek Comfort:** Embrace the journey, even the uncomfortable shifts, for they lead to growth and success.

- **Crucial Investments:** Invest time in developing both you and your team, for their success is your success as a leader. Growth is your best weapon to stay relevant.

- **Leadership is Not About Being the Best:** It's about bringing out the best in others. It's a commitment to inspiring and empowering others to achieve their greatest potential. A true leader understands that their success is measured not by their individual accomplishments, but by the growth and triumphs of those they lead.

- **Courage is Where it All Begins:** So, go ahead—be the first one on the dance floor, metaphorically or otherwise. Your team is waiting for the beat.

CHAPTER 6:
THE ACCIDENTAL LEADER — A TALE OF EARLY BLUNDERS & WINS

In my twenties, I stumbled into my first high-tech role as a project manager, and just like that, the accidental leader was again called to action.

It wasn't glamorous, and it sure wasn't planned—one day, I was happily designing, debugging, and deploying automatic guided vehicle systems; the next, I was expected to lead a team of talented engineers without a clue as to what I was doing.

I was great at my functional specialty, but my leadership skills? Let's just say they were... *a work in progress.*

My leadership style worked like a charm for half the team, while the other half looked like they were auditioning for a sequel to *Office Space*. Some of these brilliant engineers were getting left behind, and it was clear I needed to step up my game. If I wanted to stay in a position of influence, I had to figure out this whole "leadership" thing—and fast.

Learning to Lead: The Carrot Over the Stick (and Why That's Still Not Enough)

In a Chinese proverb, it is said, "A journey of a thousand miles begins with a single step." And let me tell you, developing leadership skills felt like trekking across a desert barefoot.

I quickly learned that dangling a carrot instead of wielding a stick was a great way to get people moving in the right direction. But if I wanted to inspire my team to run the marathon with me, not just crawl across the finish line, I had to do more than offer the occasional carrot. I had to become a real leader—whatever that meant.

The Quest for Wisdom: My Misadventures in Leadership Literature

With the urgency of someone studying for finals the night before, I dove headfirst into every business journal, magazine, and book I could find on how to be a great manager.

Spoiler alert: most of them were awful.

Remember those old leadership books? They were like reading a recipe for success written by someone who has never cooked a day in their life.

Some authors seemed to think that hiring a secretary was equivalent to managing a team, and others were stuck in the ivory tower of academia, dispensing advice with all the warmth of a textbook.

I grew up reading works by Kouzes and Posner—great for theory, but a bit too "ivory tower" for my taste.

Tom Peters? Brilliant but bordering on the psychotic and now completely obsolete.

And then there was Jack Welch, the king of cutthroat tactics. If you wanted to manage like it was *Survivor: Corporate Edition*, he was your guy. But genuine leadership? Not so much.

Even Jim Collins' *Good to Great* was built on data compiled by grad students and TAs—data-rich, sure, but it missed the real-world grit and grind of business leadership.

My journey was like trying to learn to swim by reading about it—helpful, but not the same as diving into the deep end and trying not to drown.

The Laughable Advice That Didn't Help (And the Rare Gems That Did)

At one point, a mentor suggested I read *The Art of War* to evolve my leadership skills to a whole new level. *The Art of War?* As if leading a team of engineers were a covert military operation. Let's just say it was almost laughable.

And don't get me started on the twenty-three-year-old "life coaches" who aspire to teach others how to be successful. Nothing like getting success advice from someone whose biggest accomplishment was getting their mom to pack them a healthy lunch.

But amid the noise, there were some rare gems of advice that did help me along the way.

True leadership, I learned, isn't about who controls the purse strings or who can instill the most fear; it's about bringing out the best in people.

It's about making people want to give their best because they believe in what they're doing, and they believe you're the one who can help them get there.

It wasn't all doom and gloom. In 2000, I took a course that studied John C. Maxwell's *21 Irrefutable Laws of Leadership*. For roughly six months, we dissected one chapter a week, and let me tell you—it was hands down the best leadership training experience that I've ever had.

Each session felt like uncovering another secret ingredient to the leadership recipe I'd been missing.

Now, remember how I struggled to influence 100 percent of my teammates? (Yes, even that one guy who always showed up late to meetings.) Well, this revealed the secrets that had eluded me.

In short, this course was a game-changer. It opened my eyes to the power of servant-style leadership, where it's not just about leading from the front, but ensuring no one gets left behind.

Turns out, leading isn't about dragging people along; it's about inspiring them to walk with you.

Stepping Beyond Comfort: Embracing the Call to Adventure

Another favorite early leadership book was *Shackleton's Way*.

It captures that unique human urge to explore. The story shared one of the boldest and wackiest want ads in history.

In 1912, the legendary British Antarctic explorer Ernest Shackleton posted the following ad in a London paper:

"MEN WANTED FOR HAZARDOUS JOURNEY. SMALL WAGES, BITTER COLD, LONG MONTHS OF COMPLETE DARKNESS, CONSTANT DANGER,

SAFE RETURN DOUBTFUL. HONOR AND RECOGNITION IN THE CASE OF SUCCESS."

You'd think that would have sent people running for the hills, but it reportedly drew over 5,000 applicants! Shackleton wasn't selling comfort; he was selling a shot at something extraordinary—a chance to be part of an adventure that would test every ounce of their grit and endurance. He was selling a dream.

In 1914, Shackleton and his team embarked on their fateful journey to the South Pole. Things didn't go as planned (understatement of the century). Their ship was trapped and crushed by the relentless Antarctic ice, and they faced months of bitter cold, isolation, and constant danger.

Every man was forced to confront unthinkable conditions, ultimately discovering the depths of his own strength and resilience.

They never reached the South Pole, but here's the thing: they all survived. Shackleton delivered on his promise of "honor and recognition"—their names live on, etched forever in history, as testaments to human endurance.

Few tales better capture our need to explore, to challenge ourselves, and to reach for something greater than we thought possible.

Stepping outside our comfort zone might not involve Antarctic ice and darkness, but it has its own set of challenges. Growth doesn't come from sitting still. It comes from those moments when we risk short-term comfort for long-term gain, when we swap the familiar for the unknown.

Sure, it can be a little scary, and there's usually no guarantee of success. But the rewards—the personal growth, the resilience, the knowledge that you dared to reach beyond the familiar—are worth it.

So, if you're feeling that itch to push the boundaries, take a page from Shackleton's story. It may not be comfortable, but it just might be extraordinary.

The future belongs to those who are willing to trade comfort for adventure, who are ready to brave a little "hazardous journey" for the promise of something greater.

The Alchemy of Caring: My Journey to Authentic Leadership

My journey toward becoming a transformational leader has been deeply personal, filled with more than a few detours and dead ends. But one thing has always been clear: caring is the currency of the team. When people know you care, they care too. It's as simple (and as difficult) as that.

Over the years, I've gleaned insights that transcend the mundane checklists and buzzwords of typical leadership literature.

I've learned that being a leader isn't about telling people what to do; it's about showing them why it matters. It's an awe-inspiring responsibility and a tremendous privilege— and, yes, sometimes it's a bit of a circus act. But when you get it right, there's nothing quite like it.

True leadership isn't about controlling purse strings or instilling fear; it's about bringing out the best in others. It's an awe-inspiring responsibility and a tremendous privilege.

My own journey toward transformational leadership has been deeply personal and uniquely relevant. Through navigating the maze of leadership literature, I've gleaned insights that transcend the mundane and embrace the essence of authentic leadership.

Caring is the currency of the team.

Key Points

- **Leadership Is a Learning Journey:** Stepping into a leadership role often starts without a clear road map. The journey involves continuous learning, and early mistakes are part of the process. Developing leadership skills requires more than just technical expertise.

- **Conventional Leadership Books Often Fall Short:** Many leadership resources are too theoretical, outdated, or written without real-world experience. While some books can provide valuable insights, aspiring leaders must sift through a lot of ineffective advice to find what truly resonates.

- **True Leadership Isn't About Power or Control:** Authentic leadership is not about wielding authority, controlling budgets, or instilling fear. It's about inspiring and bringing out the best in people, creating a positive environment where everyone feels motivated to succeed.

- **Caring Is the Core of Effective Leadership:** The most critical element of successful leadership is genuinely caring about the people you lead. When team members know their leader cares, it inspires trust, loyalty, and a shared commitment to achieving goals.

The Evolving Leader

In my late teens, leadership responsibilities came my way—whether I wanted them or not.

If there was a job to be done, I was often appointed the team lead, supervisor, or manager. On almost every occasion, I was surprised.

As mentioned, my first job out of college was at Apogee Robotics, designing Automatic Guided Vehicle Systems (AGVs) and industrial automation. By the end of my first year, I found myself leading technical teams.

By the end of my second year with the company, I went into project management.

These leadership patterns persisted, prompting me to reflect on my first management role at Hewlett-Packard (HP), a Fortune 50 company.

We were productizing an innovative technology out of HP Labs for the new hand-held scanner (aka CapShare 910/e-copier). We were innovating technologies for optical navigation on paper products—the optical mouse—the killer technology that ultimately replaced the painful track roller ball technologies in the computer mouse.

The journey was epic and serendipitous.

The Optical Odyssey—Enter the Mouse's Lair

Welcome to the whimsical world of engineering leadership, where the task at hand is to lead a brilliant team of engineers through the labyrinth of designing an optical navigation system.

Yes, you heard it right—we're talking about the unsung hero of the PC world—the optical mouse!

All across the computing world, the bane of the track roller ball mouse plagued our everyday efforts. Luckily, there was a technology innovated in the bowels of HP Labs that could look at the paper optically and navigate across the surface with precision.

Our journey started in a corporate conference room, where the smell of fresh whiteboard markers and the sound of scribbling equations filled the air.

Our mission, should we choose to accept it, was to create an electro-optical beast that could capture the very essence of cursor movement—and let me tell you, it was no Mickey Mouse operation. It was a blend of mechanical, optical, electrical, firmware, and software engineers gathered together with only one goal in mind—to navigate paper without the flaky roller ball technology.

Armed with nothing but our wits and an endless supply of caffeine, we embarked on the great blueprint bonanza. Diagrams were drawn, components were listed, and somewhere along the way, someone suggested we use a hamster wheel for harnessing free energy.

We laughed, we cried, we accidentally created a blueprint for a toaster—but eventually, we had our designs.

With our blueprints in hand, we danced the tinkerer's tango. There were wires everywhere, soldering irons became our wands, and circuit boards our canvas.

We were artists, and resistance wasn't futile—it was necessary for our calculations.

Then came the code conundrum. Lines upon lines of programming that would make even the most seasoned coder's head spin. "If" statements nested like Russian dolls, and "for-loops" spun faster than our heads after the third pot of coffee.

The moment of truth arrived with the test trials. Our creation, which we had lovingly dubbed "R2," was ready to show us what it was made of. It was a symphony of wires, power supplies, instruments, and five circuit boards tied into the open architecture I/O bus of an IBM PC.

We held our breath as the first full-frame image was extracted, and it was… a blurry blob. Back to the drawing board!

After what seemed like an eternity (but was actually a few more long days, late nights, and weekends), we had our eureka moment. A tweak here, a calibration there, and suddenly, R2 was capturing images like a pro.

We had done it—we had effectively extracted the very first real-time video image out of our mouse's silicon and had serendipitously engineered the next-generation platform of the optical mouse.

As we basked in the glow of our monitors, we realized that we had not only designed an instrument of precision but also forged a team that could tackle any challenge, as long as it didn't involve actual mice, because let's be honest, they're kind of unpredictable.

So, there you have it, folks—the tale of how a team of intrepid engineers conquered the optical odyssey.

It was shortly thereafter that I was promoted from technical lead and principal electrical engineer to the new engineering manager of the optical navigation and imaging solutions team for the innovative line of new HP products.

Once again, I was the accidental leader.

The moral of the story? Never underestimate the power of a good mouse joke to keep the spirits high and the creativity flowing.

If you are an accidental leader or an aspiring leader, this journey is for you.

Disclaimer: No actual mice (or hamsters) were used in the making of this optical navigation proof of concept. All characters appearing in this work are fictitious. Any resemblance to real people, living or dead, is purely coincidental.

PART II

---

6 TENETS OF THE ALCHEMIST'S WAY

- The 3 Cs of Setting Goals
- Building Belief
- Character and Integrity
- Vitality and Energy
- Daily Habits and Morning Rituals
- The Heart of the Servant Leader
- Aligning Goals to Your Purpose

CHAPTER 7: INTRODUCTION—SIX CORE TENETS OF HITTING YOUR GOALS

In early 2024, a curious trend emerged: life coaches everywhere were trumpeting the same message, *"Don't set goals."*

Like nails on a chalkboard, I cringed at the notion. It was as if the universe had collectively decided that aimless wandering was the new key to success. Now, they had their reasons— something about avoiding the pressure, stress, and inevitable guilt that comes when goals aren't met.

But as someone who has spent decades working through challenges, consistently leading teams to deliver complex designs, and celebrating over 100 innovations in products and services (not to mention proudly witnessing my daughter's recent graduation in engineering), this idea didn't sit right with me.

Without goals, none of those accomplishments would have been possible.

The Science Behind Goal Setting

The idea that setting goals is detrimental ignores decades

of research that shows the opposite.

Numerous studies have demonstrated that having clear goals significantly improves a person's life satisfaction and performance across various domains.

According to Dr. Damon Burton from the University of Idaho, people who set goals report being significantly happier, suffering less anxiety, and exhibiting better concentration. They also enjoy improved self-confidence, higher efficiency, and consistently perform better than those who don't set clear objectives.

Another case for setting goals: "According to a study by Dr. Gail Matthews, published in an American Psychological Association journal, individuals who wrote down their goals and reviewed them regularly were found to be 42% more likely to achieve them compared to those who did not write down their goals."

The act of goal setting not only enhances clarity and focus but also creates a sense of purpose, which fuels motivation and drives perseverance.

Goal Setting: The Framework for Success

It's no secret that the most successful individuals and organizations set clear, measurable goals.

Think of any major achievement, whether it's launching a successful product, completing a marathon, or even earning an engineering degree—it all starts with a clear, concise, and compelling goal.

Goals provide direction, helping us navigate through the chaos of distractions and uncertainties.

They act like a GPS, guiding us through detours, setbacks, and unexpected turns until we reach our destination.

For me, goals have been the cornerstone of every major accomplishment in my career and personal life. They kept me grounded and focused, especially during challenging times.

For example, after a spectacular motorcycle accident left me with a long road to recovery, I set clear fitness goals (my "trifecta"—more on that later) that helped me regain strength and confidence on my road to recovery.

Without those goals, it would have been easy to get lost in distractions or overwhelmed by the enormity of the challenge.

The Real Danger: Drifting Without Direction

The trend to avoid setting goals in favor of "going with the flow" overlooks the real danger: drifting without direction.

Without clear goals, how do we know what we're aiming for? How do we measure progress?

It's a bit like trying to build a bridge without a blueprint—you'll end up wasting time, energy, and resources, and you still might not make it to the other side.

In the workplace, clear goals are what separate high-performing teams from those that just "do their job."

If setting goals can dramatically improve outcomes in a professional environment, why would it be any different for personal growth?

Goals: A Source of Motivation and Satisfaction

Setting and achieving goals isn't just about reaching the

finish line; it's about the journey and the satisfaction that comes from making progress.

When you set a goal and see yourself moving toward it, your brain releases dopamine, a chemical that makes you feel good. This not only boosts your mood but also reinforces the behavior, making it more likely that you'll continue striving for your goals.

Goals provide the opportunity to celebrate small victories along the way. Whether it's hitting a fitness milestone, completing a challenging project, or watching my daughter walk across the stage at her engineering graduation, each achievement builds momentum. It's like collecting puzzle pieces that slowly but surely form a complete picture.

The Winner Effect: Small Wins, Big Impact

As mentioned, each time you set a goal and make progress toward it, your brain releases a feel-good chemical that gives you a little victory boost.

This isn't just psychological fluff; it's a scientifically backed phenomenon called the "Winner Effect." Each small win triggers dopamine, making you more motivated, more focused, and more confident. Essentially, setting and achieving goals creates a positive feedback loop that builds momentum, like a snowball rolling downhill. That's why winning Super Bowl teams keep winning Super Bowls.

The beauty of the Winner Effect is that it can turn an average Monday into a celebration if you've set achievable milestones.

Goals: The Alchemical Backbone

Goals have been the backbone of my journey, and that's what compelled me to organize these thoughts into *The Alchemist's Way*.

You see, *The Alchemist's Way* isn't just about setting goals; it's about setting them properly, pursuing them, and achieving them in a way that feels natural, fulfilling, and, yes, even fun.

I wanted to create a framework where all the essential aspects of leadership could harmonize to help you accelerate your journey to attainment, because let's be honest, we're all on a journey, and no one wants to feel like they're stuck on a treadmill going nowhere.

The six core tenets of leadership that we'll explore in the next chapters aren't just a list of "do this, not that." Think of them as a framework for success that serves as guiding principles that turn chaos into clarity, confusion into confidence, and, if you allow a little magic, lead into gold.

I know that last one sounds a bit fantastical, but hey, it's *The Alchemist's Way*, and we're here to make the extraordinary happen.

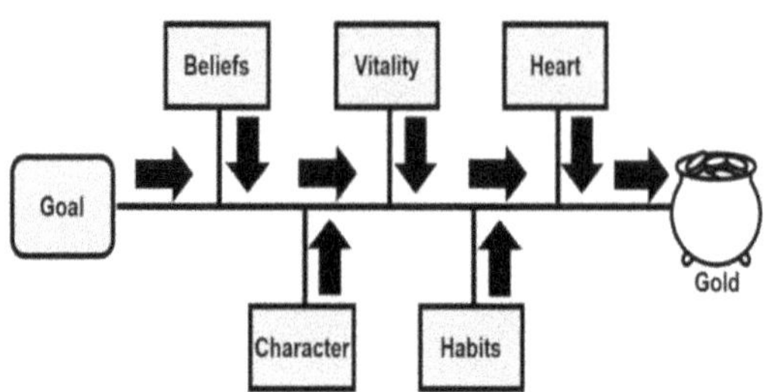

Embrace the Power of Goals

So, while some may advocate for a more relaxed, goal-free approach to life, I believe the power of setting clear, concise, and compelling goals is essential. Goals give us a sense of purpose, direct our energy, and allow us to measure progress. They turn dreams into actionable plans and provide the structure needed to navigate life's challenges.

Don't just set goals; set big, scary, exciting goals that make you want to jump out of bed in the morning.

After all, the greatest satisfaction often comes not from the destination but from knowing that you had the courage to aim high and the determination to keep moving forward, one step at a time.

So, in the next six chapters, we'll delve into the heart of these tenets. We'll look at how to set goals that inspire rather than intimidate, how to lead with a balance of strategy and intuition, and how to navigate the ups and downs with the grace of someone who's got this whole "leadership" thing figured out.

Spoiler alert: No one's got it completely figured out, but with these six tenets, you'll feel a lot closer to purposeful wins.

So, grab your notebook, your favorite pen, and maybe even a cup of coffee (trust me, it helps), and let's dive into the alchemy of goal setting.

CHAPTER 8:
The Alchemy of Goal Setting — The Secret 3 C's

Imagine the Alchemist meticulously crafting a blueprint, ensuring clarity in every detail. In personal mastery and leadership, goals are the blueprint, and the Alchemist crafts them with precision, clear, concise, and irresistibly compelling.

In the ancient alchemical forge of leadership, the first principle in goal setting that emerges from the crucible is the essence of the 3 C's.

A well-stated goal must have the following:

- **Compelling**
- **Clear**
- **Concise**

As the Alchemist views the molten potential of lead, so does the leader perceive nebulous goals and projects, knowing that their transformative potential lies in the clarity of articulation.

Compelling as Enchantment

The first C of goal setting is compelling.

An alchemical transformation must be alluring, drawing the beholder into its mystic allure. So, it is with our goals—they are not just objectives but compelling visions that captivate our hearts and minds.

Whether you are leading yourself to a better life or leading a team, human nature doesn't blindly follow our destiny unless we are enchanted by the allure of a compelling goal.

Compelling goals are like the smell of fresh coffee in the morning, irresistibly drawing us out of bed, even when the bed is arguing quite convincingly for a few more minutes of sleep.

Proper goal setting is the holy grail of productivity!

Let me illustrate. Does gravity ask the apple for permission before making it fall from the tree to the ground? No, compelling goals don't wait for our approval to pull us toward them.

Consider the magnet—does it negotiate with the paper clip as to which direction it should move? No. Similarly, a compelling goal doesn't entertain our excuses. It simply says, "Hey, I'm over here! Stop scrolling through social media and start moving!"

Compelling goals get us off the couch and pull us, like gravity, toward them.

The greater the goal, the easier it becomes to endure discomfort and overcome barriers. When properly chosen, they thrust you out of your comfort zone, so dream big and go after that big goal!

In essence, compelling goals are the ultimate puppet masters, pulling our strings and making us dance to the tune of progress and achievement. And the best part? We're more than happy to bust a move!

> *"Set a goal to achieve something that is so big, so exhilarating that it excites you and scares you at the same time."*
>
> **— Bob Proctor**

One of my favorite exercises is goal setting. Do you know why I love it so much? It's because I keep making it bigger and bigger until it scares me. I often reflect on these sage words…

Set BIG goals.

Dream Big.

Think Big.

Don't be afraid to take risks.

Use your talents.

Make the most of yourself.

Don't give up. Keep going. Keep at it.

Don't compare yourself to others.

Just compare yourself to yourself and strive to be better each day.

Do something that is significant.

Something that adds value and meaning to your life, and the lives of others.

—Ken Blanchard

Challenge

How do we make sure that our goals are compelling? One of the processes that I use is as follows:

A compelling goal is more than just an objective; it's a vision so captivating that it pulls you toward it with the force of gravity. It enchants the heart and mind, motivating you to act even when resistance tempts you to stay still.

Like the aroma of fresh coffee that gets you out of bed, compelling goals don't wait for permission—they ignite a desire to move forward, breaking through comfort zones and overcoming obstacles.

The magic of a compelling goal lies in its ability to inspire and sustain effort. It must excite you, challenge you, and, as Bob Proctor suggests, scare you just enough to push you toward growth. Dream big, think big, and set goals that draw out your best self.

Steps to Create a Compelling Goal

1. **Relax and Reflect:** Use meditation or calming techniques to center yourself.
2. **Brainstorm Freely:** Set a timer for 20 minutes and write down as many goals as you can. Don't stop or overthink— keep the pen moving!

3. **Pause:** Set the pen down and get excited about your future. Look at what you wrote.

4. **Identify the Game-Changer:** Review your list and find the one goal that stands out—the one that would change your life if achieved.

5. **Refine Your Vision:** Write it down on a clean page, along with:

- Why it matters
- The positive changes it will bring
- The consequences of not achieving it

By focusing on a goal that captivates and challenges you, you create the momentum to move toward it.

A compelling goal becomes the ultimate motivator, drawing you closer to progress and achievement.

Now that you have a compelling goal, let's go on to the second C of goal setting.

Clear as Crystal

The second C of goal setting is clarity.

Crafting clarity in our goals is akin to the delicate artistry of an alchemist, where each intention gleams as clear as the crystalline waters of a mountain spring.

Our goals shouldn't resemble wisps of fog but rather crystalline visions—sharp and precise, leaving no room for ambiguity or misunderstanding.

Clarity is the key. After all, *blurry targets don't get hit.*

Without this clarity, we wander through a fog of uncertainty, easily swayed by distractions that lead us astray.

But with clarity comes a powerful force. It's crucial to enable visualization. A clear goal ignites our imagination, fuels our focus, stirs motivation, and bolsters confidence.

With a clear goal in mind, our actions become deliberate, purposeful steps toward our desired outcome.

During planning sessions of complex designs, revisiting the vision of the end goal proves immensely beneficial. This enables team members to focus on the important tasks and see how their contributions align with the overall vision. They can visualize their fingerprints on the final masterpiece.

Speaking of masterpieces, Mount Rushmore is a colossal sculpture in South Dakota, featuring the carved faces of four U.S. presidents on a mountain. Often regarded as one of the marvels of human ingenuity, Mount Rushmore stands as a testament to vision and artistry.

Mount Rushmore is worth seeing. The reason I bring this up is that it illustrates a glowing example of casting a crystal-clear vision of the end goal for the purposes of enabling teams.

Mount Rushmore was a huge and daunting task to undertake. I admire the vision, effort, and artistry it took to create.

Gutzon Borglum, the sculptor behind Mount Rushmore, created several models of his vision, but one model stood out in my memory.

Housed at the base of the mountain is a 1/12th scale model in a rather stark building—now enshrined within a visitor's center.

Borglum employed a technique he affectionately referred to as "pointing."

Daily, the team would visit the models, instrumenting them with plumb bobs, protractors, and take precise measurements of the model. They would then multiply those measurements by twelve and climb the mountain to transpose their artistry into the granite.

Today, you can behold that awesome result as one of the greatest man-made wonders of the world.

For the Alchemist, clarity is more than a tool—it's a sculptor's chisel, shaping nebulous concepts into tangible pathways. It's about illuminating the journey ahead, guiding each team member toward a shared vision.

As Warren Bennis aptly noted, *"In order to serve its purpose, a vision has to be a shared vision."*

Clarity ensures that every member of the team sees not only the destination but also the path to get there.

With clarity as our compass, we navigate through distractions and uncertainties, holding steadfast to our vision of success. It's the lifeline that keeps us tethered to our goals, even in the midst of chaos and confusion.

So, let us embrace clarity as our guiding light, illuminating the way forward and propelling us toward our dreams with unwavering resolve and purpose. After all, in a world filled with distractions, clarity is our North Star, guiding us home to the fulfillment of our aspirations. So, clarity of our goals is essential to attainment.

Now that you have your goal and can visualize it with absolute clarity, you're ready for the final C of goal setting—Concise.

Concise as a Masterpiece

The third and final C of goal setting is concise.

With all the distractions in the modern world, conciseness is essential to deliver us from the barrage of our daily distractions.

In the Alchemist's domain, efficiency is an art. Similarly, the Alchemist weaves a concise narrative for goals—a masterpiece of brevity cuts through the noise.

With every unnecessary word removed, the goal shines as a beacon, guiding the way with succinct brilliance.

Brevity is key in goal setting. I distill my goals into virtual mantras, and I infuse them with emotion for maximum impact. It's my winning recipe for attainment!

Lessons in Resilience

In 2007, I had a motorcycle accident so spectacular that Evel Knievel would have been jealous.

Unfortunately, it left me devastatingly broken, but the tragedy didn't stop there.

My life was met with the perfect storm of catastrophe. While I was in the throes of healing and knee reconstruction, my wife of almost ten years decided to exit stage left.

All at once, everything that defined me seemed to disappear. My strength, my wife, my family, my confidence, my marriage, my money, my spirit, my zest for life, and my identity as both an athlete and a family man— all vanished faster than a magician's rabbit.

It felt like the universe had pulled the rug out from under me, leaving me to figure out who I was without the roles I had cherished.

To make matters even more devastating, for the next several years, I only had half-time custody of my beautiful daughter, Alexa. Those years were tough, filled with heartache and longing, but they also became a testament to our bond.

When she was so little, I put her to bed at night with epic tales of princesses, knights, grand adventures, and faraway kingdoms, each story wrapping up with a loving prayer.

In the mornings, she'd pop up at dawn, tiptoe into our room, and whisper in my ear, "Daddy, are you awake?" Those words were better than any alarm clock and catapulted me out of bed for a beautiful start to my day.

Divorce meant losing 50 percent of those precious nights and mornings, and it was more than my soul could take.

I was desperate and devastated, staring down the deep well of my own loss.

Yeah, this transition, this loss—it convinced me that I'd received a one-way ticket to my own private "death sentence." I couldn't shake the feeling that God was using me for His own episode of *The Book of Job 2.0: The Sequel.*

My soul, spirit, confidence, and family were all MIA, and I was left feeling like I'd been hit with a double whammy of divine tough love.

The injuries from the motorcycle accident were a constellation of shattered bones around my left knee (others as well), but these injuries put an abrupt end to my sports-related activities like jogging, tennis, racquetball, and, well, anything that involved moving. It was quite literally the perfect storm of disaster.

Years later, Alexa reached her teens, and everything changed.

Alexa was able to live with me full-time. In that moment, my world felt whole again. She was, and always will be, my greatest source of joy and the glue that put my shattered pieces back together.

Alexa was my purpose in life. She needed me, and I couldn't have been prouder of the way that our tiny and strong family evolved, healthy and happy.

Even though I was missing out on my engagement in sports, Alexa was with me, and I was striding toward new goals and adventures (albeit with a limp in my gait).

During those years, I had learned to be a single dad, learned how to cook well, how to nurture like a mom (family, friends, and my daughter gave me Mother's Day cards in addition to Father's Day cards—oofda, talk about taking a punch off my "man-card"), how to entertain alone, live alone, be alone, and be a great dad to a lovely daughter alone.

The Knee that Turned Three: A Playful Journey of Renewed Mobility

After years of suffering, I finally accepted that it was time for a new knee, so I headed to the best clinic in Vail, CO, to get a shiny, state-of-the-art replacement.

Last holiday season arrived with a unique milestone—my knee officially turned three years old. That spectacular motorcycle accident back in 2007 was finally coming to a close.

These days, I joke that my knee is the youngest part of me, still a toddler, and like any three-year-old, it has its moods. Sometimes it's a little stiff, and I imagine it sulking, like, "Do we really have to do stairs today?"

Other times, it's bouncing along happily, ready to show off. But every now and then, when it creaks just a bit, I swear it's whispering, *"Remember that time you thought a motorcycle stunt was a great idea?"*

With a touch of humor, I proudly declare that my new knee not only restored my mobility but somehow managed to turn back the clock, lowering the average age of my body with these new parts.

Yes, I was celebrating the proud ownership of a toddler knee, navigating its milestones from post-surgery recovery to newfound flexibility and strength. As I step (pardon the pun) into another holiday season, I'm reflecting on the gift of humor in the face of adversity and the courage to embrace change.

My knee, a testament to modern medical marvels, has become a playful symbol of renewal, not just physically, but in the broader context of life.

This knee has given me a fresh start, and yes, it's even brought some humor back into my life.

My knee might be three, but today it's more flexible than my schedule. It's like having a toddler that doesn't throw tantrums but helps me keep up with a daily step count. Who knew that a piece of metal could be such a playful symbol of renewal?

A Few Thoughts on My Knee's Playful Journey:

- "My new knee has lowered the average age of my body."
- "They say a knee replacement is a step in the right direction—I'm counting almost 10K steps a day for nearly three years now!"
- "Why did the knee go to therapy? It had too many issues to *kneed* to work through!"

The Journey to Recovery and the Birth of the Trifecta

After the knee replacement, I set a simple, powerful goal: regain the strength I had in my forties and reach a specific weight. This goal had three parts:

- Bench 225 lbs.
- Squat 225 lbs.

- Weigh 225 lbs.

I called it *"The Trifecta,"* a triumvirate built around the number 225.

Every morning, before I hit the gym, stepped on the scale, or went for a walk, I would assertively speak *"Trifecta."* Every time I said that word, I linked it with strong emotion and a clear vision of its attainment. That one word became my mantra, my rallying cry, and it drove me every single day for nearly twenty months until I achieved it.

The Power of a Mantra: The Trifecta in Action

Mantras are more than just catchy words—they're the embodiment of clarity and focus. *"Trifecta"* worked because it was concise, powerful, and easy to remember. It wasn't bogged down with details or distractions.

It was a laser beam cutting through my mental clutter, reminding me exactly what I was working toward every day.

A succinct mantra isn't just for fitness; it's a formula that can work for any goal.

Do you want to stick to exercising 12 times a month? Call it *"The Dirty Dozen"*—a little grit, a lot of determination. Aiming to average 10,000 steps a day? Try *"The Sovereign 10"*—you'll walk like royalty. Need to stay under 2000 calories daily? Chant *"OK 2K today"*—because if your calories are in check, you'll be okay.

Over the years, teams have crafted acronyms to create succinct, smart mantras. These have been invaluable for maintaining project focus and adding fun to program management.

Consider Applying This Principle to Your Own Goals:

- STRONG – Sweat, Train, Rest, Overcome, Nourish, Grow
- MOVE – Make Opportunities Value Effort
- FAST – Fuel, Act, Sweat, Thrive

These compact, memorable mantras can serve as your personal guideposts for progress and success. Which one will you create or claim as your own?

A good mantra is short, simple, and brimming with energy. It's like a sticky note for your brain, but one that you can shout in the mirror with a bit of flair.

It's not just about words; it's about crafting a rallying cry that connects with your emotions and keeps your goals front and center.

Clarity and Simplicity: The Leadership Alchemist's Wand

The Alchemist's wand may be the wordsmith's pen in the Leadership Alchemist's hand, but it's precision and clarity that turn dreams into reality.

When goals are simple, they don't just live in your head—they embed themselves in your actions, becoming part of your identity.

Dream big, live large, and grow into the person who makes those dreams a reality. After all, the clearer the goal, the easier it is to take the first step, and to keep stepping until you arrive.

So, whether your mantra is *"Trifecta," "Dirty Dozen,"* or even *"Don't Eat the Chips,"* make it yours.

Say it loud, say it often, and let it carry you forward.

Dream big, live large, and grow into the person who makes those dreams come true!

Key Points

- **The 3 Cs of Goal Setting:** Compelling, Clear, and Concise—each one as essential as the ingredients in a successful alchemical transformation.

- **Compelling Goals Don't Negotiate with Your Comfort:** They pull you toward them, like a magnet.

- **Clear Goals Are Like Mount Rushmore:** Crystal clear from the start, built to withstand distractions and fog.

- **Trim the Fat**: Keep your goals concise and turn them into mantras fused with emotion, and they will drive you into action every day.

CHAPTER 9:
THE ALCHEMY OF BELIEF—BUILDING BELIEF IN THE GOAL

Just as the Alchemist's belief in the transformative process is paramount, we must instill unwavering belief in the outcomes ahead, catalyzing the magical transformation from doubt to determination.

In the realm of *The Alchemist's Way*, the second principle reveals itself: **belief**.

Over the years, my daughter Alexa faced many discouraging comments aimed at dissuading her from pursuing engineering as a career. Some said, "Engineering isn't for girls," or "You should become an artist because you like to draw, or a veterinarian because you like dogs." One of the harshest remarks came from a peer who said,

"Engineering is tough. You have to know what you are doing, or you'd better go home and play with your Barbies."

These words planted seeds of doubt in Alexa and triggered her overly protective father.

It took immense effort and encouragement to rewrite the negative narratives swirling around her. That internal battle is powerful—self-talk can be the most potent dream killer.

One of the biggest obstacles to faith sits right between our ears—our own mind.

As Arnold Schwarzenegger said, "The mind is the limit. As long as the mind can envision that you can do something, you can do it, as long as you really believe 100 percent." By extension, the mind is also our greatest enabler. But to truly grasp this, you'll need to summon some unshakable faith in the unknown. If you believe in your vision with conviction, you're already halfway to achieving it.

Schwarzenegger also said, "What you do is create a vision of who you want to be, and then live into that picture as if it were already true." Think of it as acting out your own mental movie in which you're the star—and spoiler alert: you succeed!

Positive visualization isn't just a feel-good exercise; it's a tool used by champions in every field. Olympic athletes, musicians, dancers, CEOs—they all harness visualization to build faith and confidence before they step up to perform.

When it comes to your goals, start picturing yourself there. After all, if it's good enough for Schwarzenegger and Olympians, it's good enough for the rest of us!

Watch the Self-Talk

Research by the National Science Foundation shows we have between 12,000 and 60,000 thoughts a day. Eighty percent of them are negative, and 95 percent of those thoughts are repetitive.

Imagine the impact if we let these thoughts win.

When we face big, audacious goals, often that inner voice of fear whispers, "You can't do it, you're not enough." But then belief strides in, with mask and cape billowing, and says, "You are more than enough, and we've got this!"

Beliefs are our shield against this negativity. Whether external or internal, doubt can be crippling.

But belief is the bouncer of the mind, ready to kick fear out and keep the party going.

When we believe in the possibility of success, we set a self-fulfilling prophecy in motion. Our actions align with our thoughts, and this synergy propels us toward our vision. Belief not only steers us toward our goals but also helps us overcome the inevitable obstacles that arise.

The Bible says it best: *"Now faith is the substance of things hoped for, the evidence of things not seen."* Faith is the preview to the life we seek, just as an Alchemist must believe in the process of transformation before it can occur.

The Alchemist utilizes faith to create the vision for the desired outcome. Without vision, goal attainment would be more complex than assembling IKEA furniture without a manual.

That little voice inside of our heads is an endless tape of negative messages. No wonder so few can reach their goals or step into their destiny.

For the Alchemist, faith and belief provide a preview of the goal, just as Olympic athletes spend hours training and some even longer visualizing their successful outcome. Belief is the alchemical catalyst for success.

Let me share a couple of short stories.

Believe and Achieve

From Humble Beginnings to Tech Leadership: A Journey of Grit and Grace

Just as an Alchemist's belief in the transformative process is key to success, the Leadership Alchemist must instill unwavering belief in the outcomes ahead. This is the secret elixir that catalyzes the magical transformation from doubt to determination.

A mentor shared a great story of resilience, drawn from a truly empowering belief. Here's a paraphrased narrative of this compelling tale of resilience:

Amid a perfect storm, a once-thriving business owner found his company on the brink of collapse. Lost clients, barren pipelines, and relentless creditors painted a bleak picture of impending bankruptcy.

Feeling utterly dejected, the business owner sought solace in a nearby park and sat on a lonely park bench, contemplating the uncertain future that lay ahead.

Still unable to escape his woes, the despondent business owner sat in deep thought on that park bench, contemplating his future, knowing that his company was failing, he was flat broke, and their collective future looked glum.

He felt massively dejected.

While sitting on the bench, reflecting on his troubles, he was approached by an old man who said, "You look troubled," so the businessman shared his story with the old man.

After a long pause, the old man said, "I can help."

With that, he drew his checkbook from his coat and wrote a check, handing it to the businessman.

The businessman took the check and was aghast to see that it was for $500,000!

It was nothing short of a miracle for the failing businessman, and the money provided a beacon of hope for the future of his company.

It was a miraculous turn of fate for the struggling businessman, for that check held the promise of rescuing his failing enterprise.

Grateful and hopeful, he accepted the check and shouted, "Thank you! How can I repay you?" The old man turned around and said, "One year from today, let's meet at this park bench, and you can repay me then."

Returning to his office, he gazed at the check once again. To his disbelief, he noticed that it was signed by **John D. Rockefeller.**

The businessman had returned with a newfound fire and gathered his teams.

Months passed, marked by relentless negotiations with creditors and building bold proposals that ultimately secured unprecedented contracts.

The company, once teetering on the edge of oblivion, now stood on the cusp of resurgence, buoyed by the courage and tenacity born from a seemingly miraculous encounter.

A year passed, and as promised, the businessman returned to that park bench, and he waited... waited... and waited some more...

In the early afternoon, a small figure appeared in the distance and was slowly ambling toward the park bench.

As the figure got closer, he recognized the old man. When he rushed to reacquaint himself and share the great news of his business success, the old man leaned forward with a look of confusion. The businessman was wondering if the old man even remembered him.

In a few moments, a nurse came running up and cradled the old man's arm and said, "There you are," and she turned to the businessman and said, "I am sorry if he was a bother to you. He tends to wander off and tell people that he is the wealthy financial tycoon, John D. Rockefeller."

All at once, he realized that he had been deceived. The check, of course, was worthless.

…But then again… was it?

Despite the check's invalidity, it had become a symbolic safety net—a source of hope, inspiration, and motivation to try again.

Safely tucked away, the mere presence of the check emboldened him to take massive risks, negotiate fiercely, and drive new sales to revive his business.

This story speaks to the alchemy of belief—sometimes, the greatest treasure lies not in external resources, but in our belief that propels us forward.

This story made me reflect on my own story of *"Believe and Achieve."*

My own journey is a testament to this power. Growing up in humble circumstances, I learned to work hard at a young age. By age twelve, I was earning my own way, and by eighteen, I had set out for my epic Viking saga down the engineering trail.

Was engineering the right answer? Well, at the time, it was better than many of the other paths under consideration.

Money and resources were scarce, but belief was abundant.

I struggled through college, often lacking resources, experience, and guidance, but my unwavering belief in my vision carried me through.

My life story is a testament to the unwavering spirit that can emerge from an origin of humble beginnings.

Raised in circumstances where financial struggles were a constant companion, life demanded that I mature faster than most, and far faster than I would have preferred.

My dad had two rules for all four of his kids:

- "You're moving out when you're eighteen."
- "Never borrow money from me."

To put it mildly, it was a wake-up call and my crash course into adulthood.

Enter the Graduate

As mentioned, I navigated the challenging terrain of engineering school, financing my education through hard work and sheer determination.

College was a struggle and a crucible where the fires of ambition and financial hardship forged a resolve that would carry me through the years to come.

After graduating with a BSEE, I set out to move to Colorado and find that tiny A-frame cabin on a beautiful mountain lake.

As a new graduate, I was emotionally and financially bankrupt. I had no relevant experience, and the odds of succeeding seemed insurmountable as I entered this harsh and competitive workforce.

Yet, it was precisely at this juncture that the indomitable human spirit within me emerged.

Fast forward thirty-seven years, and I stand at the helm, leading top-talent engineering teams to our collective achievement, having steered the course through numerous challenges.

The journey was nothing short of miraculous.

At the start, I lacked the resources, social skills, experience, encouragement, leadership, mentorship, and finances necessary for success. However, what I did possess was a profound belief in myself, a killer work ethic, and a vivid vision of the leader I aspired to become.

This belief acted as a catalyst, propelling me to rapidly acquire the skills, behaviors, and domain knowledge essential for success.

My story is not just one of personal triumph; it's a testament to the transformative power of determination, belief, and an unwavering vision.

Looking back, I'm immensely grateful for the journey, for it has shaped me into the leader I am today. Belief was key to enabling the outcomes that I was seeking.

Faith and belief provided the preview of the life that I wanted.

In retrospect, each challenge, every setback, and the scarcity of resources were but stepping stones on the path to success. Each challenge carried with it a serendipitous jewel of growth and strength.

My heartfelt gratitude to those who have been part of this incredible journey.

The HP Digital Entertainment Center Startup:

A Story of Belief, Grit, and Late-Night Takeout

In one of my pivotal leadership moments, I found myself championing a bold, ambitious idea: bringing HP out of the home office and into the living room.

It was a proposal brimming with transformative potential—or at least, that's what the marketing manager and I told ourselves when we pitched it.

Armed with an all-new concept and a snazzy prototype demo, we confidently presented our vision to HP's executive leadership team. To our relief (and slight surprise), they loved it.

But here's where it got interesting. After the meeting, the general manager didn't round up another group of executives to dissect the next steps. Instead, he gathered my team of engineering leaders—the people who'd actually have to bring this ambitious idea to life.

Curious, I asked him why meet the engineers?

His response was simple, but it struck a chord: "Without the engineers' belief in the project plan, this new business creation initiative would not be possible."

That was the moment I realized that no matter how great your pitch or prototype is, the real magic happens when the people building the dream believe in it.

Without their buy-in, all you have is a nice PowerPoint and a lot of wishful thinking.

And so, we rolled up our sleeves and got to work. And by "got to work," I mean *really* got to work. Late nights turned into early mornings. Weekends blurred into weekdays. There were moments it felt like the project might outlast me, or that I'd start growing roots in my office chair.

If you've ever stared at a pizza box at 2 a.m., wondering if it's judging you, you know the vibe.

But in the end, it was all worth it.

After ten grueling months (which somehow felt like decades), we launched the HP de100C, affectionately known as the Digital Entertainment Center. It wasn't just a product—it was a category-defining innovation.

It went on to win several awards for best in its class, and to this day, it's one of my favorite projects I've ever led.

Looking back, this journey wasn't just about creating a product—it was about understanding the heart of leadership. Belief isn't something you demand; it's something you earn.

The engineers didn't just build the product; they believed in it. And that belief? That's what made the impossible possible.

So, what's the takeaway?

Vision gets you in the door, but belief is what builds the house—and maybe earns you a pizza-fueled all-nighter or two along the way.

The Crucible of Transformation

In alchemy, belief is the crucible where transformation occurs. Similarly, the Alchemist understands that belief is not just a fleeting emotion but the very crucible where success is forged. Without it, the transformative process is stalled.

Dr. Maxwell Maltz said it well, "Within you right now is the power to do things you never dreamed possible. This power becomes available to you just as soon as you can change your beliefs."

The leader, like the ancient alchemists who believed in the transmutation of base metals into gold, instills unwavering belief in the team's capability. It's not just about articulating goals; it's about cultivating a shared belief in the attainability of those goals.

Belief becomes the bedrock on which success is built.

In leading advanced engineering teams, I've seen firsthand how dangerous limiting beliefs can be—they're like invisible roadblocks on the path to achievement. After years of observing this, I'm convinced: mediocre beliefs lead to mediocre results. And by the same logic, extraordinary beliefs? Well, they lead to extraordinary results.

There will always be reasons why a goal seems impossible. But when life presents us with a monumental task—one that demands heart, grit, and an unbreakable spirit—it's only an extraordinary belief that will summon the graces of the universe to make it happen. Greatness doesn't just tap anyone on the shoulder; it taps the person who believes, down to their bones, that success is within reach.

The truth is, beliefs are like muscles. They get stronger with use, and they thrive when pushed a little beyond their comfort zone. Extraordinary results come from holding extraordinary beliefs—and being willing to stand by them, even when the going gets tough.

So, let's aim high, believe boldly, and see what extraordinary things we can achieve.

Just as the Alchemist transforms base metals into gold through unwavering belief in the process, the Leadership Alchemist catalyzes the magical transformation from doubt to determination. Doubt is the lead that weighs down progress, but belief transmutes it into the gold of determination, lifting the team toward the goal.

The Alchemist works in solitude, but the Leadership Alchemist understands the power of collective belief. It's not just about personal conviction; it's about weaving a tapestry of shared belief among the team. As each team member believes in the goal and their collective ability to achieve it, the alchemical magic unfolds.

Can you picture yourself achieving, acquiring, and embracing the best that life has to offer? Surprisingly, it may be your own beliefs standing between you and your dreams.

Let's try a quick experiment: pause for a moment and create a clear mental picture of yourself. Now, stretch that vision five or ten years into the future. What are you doing?

What kind of shape are you in? Does your tomorrow look just like yesterday, or is it filled with new experiences and comforts?

Dr. Nathaniel Branden wrote in *The Six Pillars of Self-Esteem*, "Self-esteem is the disposition to experience oneself as competent to cope with the challenges of life and as deserving of happiness."

So, here's the question: do you feel deserving of happiness? Do you feel capable of tackling life's challenges head-on? Competence breeds confidence, and a sense of worthiness is often the secret ingredient in attaining life's best.

Let's take a moment for some honest self-reflection: what do you truly believe? Do you feel worthy of success? What beliefs shape your views on life, your future, or even how you interpret the world around you?

Maybe you're influenced by religion, the economy, astrology, or even the phase of the moon! Whatever your guiding forces, these beliefs matter because they set unseen boundaries that either inhibit or expand your ability to become the best version of yourself or reach that audacious goal.

Beliefs can be funny things—they're like invisible fences. We don't see them, but they quietly control the scope of what we think is possible.

The good news? You can open that fence and expand your horizons. Once you start to see yourself as fully capable and worthy of a fulfilling life, something incredible happens: a mental shift takes place that unlocks a life of possibility. You'll find yourself embracing opportunities with confidence, ready to receive the very best that life has to offer.

Let's try a shift in mindset. Do any of these thoughts sound familiar?

- "What I do doesn't matter."
- "I'm not worth fighting for."
- "I always give up on myself."
- "I'm not perfect; I can't do anything right."
- "My needs don't matter."

Consider replacing them with powerful new beliefs:

- "I was born to live a rich, meaningful life!"
- "I won't let anything hold me back!"

- "I am worth fighting for."
- "I'll let myself shine and attract success!"
- "I'm open to success and ready to celebrate it!"
- "I am excited about who I'm becoming."
- "I welcome blessings and miracles!"

Beliefs are one of the most essential elements in reaching our goals. So, here's what I'm confident in saying: you are worthy of a fulfilling life.

Self-actualization—becoming the person you're truly capable of being—is absolutely worth the effort.

Growing in character, taking risks for your dreams, and standing by your new beliefs is worth it. And, most importantly, you can become everything you imagine.

Henry Ford once said, "Whether you believe you can do a thing or not, you are right." Do you see life as a game you can win? Do you see a future where your dreams come true? My hope is that by the end of this book, you'll be saying a resounding "yes."

In this alchemical journey, the second principle—Building Belief in the Goal—is the potion that transforms doubt into determination, turning the ordinary into the extraordinary.

The Leadership Alchemist, like the ancient alchemists before, knows that belief is not just a mindset but the very alchemical agent that transmutes visions into realities.

Key Points

- **Beliefs Beat Doubt Every Time:** Beliefs are the antidote to doubt. Without them, we fall victim to negative internal and external narratives.

- **Action Enablers:** Belief aligns actions with goals. Once we believe, our efforts follow suit, setting the stage for success.

- **They Are Contagious:** Belief is contagious. If a leader believes in the goal, the team will too, and together, they can accomplish the impossible.

- **They Enable Our Vision for Success:** Faith and belief are the

alchemical catalysts for turning visions
into realities.

CHAPTER 10:
THE ALCHEMY OF CHARACTER–
TURNING CHARACTER INTO GOLD

The Alchemist's character is the crucible's purity; in leadership, integrity is the bedrock. The Alchemist values character, forging a foundation of trust that withstands the test of time.

A person's character is the greatest and hardest test of leadership, for character is both a behavior and a trait.

What is character? At its core, character is the ability to keep a promise to yourself.

Without character, we cannot influence or lead. Let me explain...

In my thirty-seven years of engineering, leading, and managing teams, I've learned that character isn't just something you're born with—it's something you forge, like steel in a furnace. It's shaped by the heat of challenges, the hammering of tough decisions, and the tempering of lessons learned through experience.

True character is built in the moments when no one is watching—when you choose integrity over shortcuts, honesty over comfort, and the right path over the easy one.

Character is the crucible that withstands the heat of pressure, challenge, and time. Without it, leadership falls apart faster than politicians' promises.

That's why, in all my years of leadership, character has been the cornerstone of my philosophy.

You can have all the strategies in the world, but if your integrity is flawed, you're not going to get very far. I often reflect on Norman Schwarzkopf's wise words: "Leadership is a potent combination of strategy and character. But if you must be without one, be without the strategy."

I've witnessed careers made and broken due to the presence or absence of character.

When character is forged in the heat of challenges and proves its strength over time, it becomes the foundation of influence and resilience.

Each trial endured not only reinforces confidence in oneself but also shapes the perception of those around you.

Your team observes, evaluates, and ultimately decides whether to place their trust in your character or not.

True leadership is built on this foundation: the unwavering consistency of character that inspires belief, even in the face of adversity. The commitment to doing the right thing ensures sustaining success.

Because without it, you're just another character in the grand sitcom of life, waiting for the laugh track to cue your exit.

With it, you're the author of your own epic saga, where every chapter is a testament to the timeless adage: honesty is indeed the best policy.

Like an Iceberg: The Depth of Character Runs Deep

During a business trip to Belfast, Ireland, I found myself gazing out the hotel window at the massive yellow cranes of the Harland & Wolff shipyard.

To my surprise, this was the very shipyard where the legendary *Titanic* was designed, built, and launched.

A visit to the local maritime museum sheds even more light on this story, revealing relics from the *Titanic's* design and construction—a poignant reminder of both human ambition and vulnerability.

In the early 1900s, the Belfast papers proudly hailed the *Titanic* as the finest, fastest, and most luxurious ocean liner in the world. Locals still take pride in her creation, including my cab driver, who was quick to defend the ship's strength, placing the blame on the unfortunate judgment of its captain rather than any flaw in design.

The *Titanic* was marketed as "unsinkable," yet on her maiden voyage, she met her match in an iceberg, taking over 1,500 lives to the bottom of the cold Atlantic. It's a tragic reminder that often what we see is just the tip of the story.

The iceberg that ended the *Titanic's* journey was barely visible above water, less than 10 percent of its actual mass. Only when the ship collided with the hidden part of this frozen giant was the true, formidable strength of the iceberg revealed.

Our relationships with people are often like the encounter between the *Titanic* and the iceberg.

We only see a small part of others, and it's easy to think that what's beneath the surface can be managed or hidden. But here's the catch: like an iceberg, character runs deep, and it always seeks to reveal itself, whether we intend for it to or not.

Life has a way of exposing our true nature, especially when we're tested.

Sometimes we may cut corners or think we can skate by without the truth showing.

Have you ever made a promise to your kids you didn't keep, fudged the story a bit to your spouse, or made an excuse at work for a job left unfinished?

The truth has a way of surfacing, and so does our integrity or lack thereof.

As Edgar J. Mohn put it, "A lie has speed, but truth has endurance."

Character, like the bulk of an iceberg, often goes unseen until we're faced with temptation, adversity, or a challenge.

Just as the *Titanic* learned, our true character is revealed in moments of collision, when life's challenges demand that we either sink or stand firm.

Character is an Investment

Developing strong character is an investment, like reinforcing a ship for the storm. It takes time, and the payoff isn't always visible right away, but when life tests us, a solid foundation of integrity is worth every ounce of effort.

If you're facing challenges in your relationships—if trust feels a little shaky—take heart. As long as we're breathing, there's time to rebuild.

Integrity is the crown jewel of success, and it's worth every bit of commitment. As D.L. Moody wisely said, "If I take care of my character, my reputation will take care of itself."

It's a simple formula, really: build the strength below the surface, and the world will see it when it matters most.

So, let's be sure we're building strong character. Because, like an iceberg, who we are underneath will always find a way to show itself. Especially when life's waters get rough, your character will serve as your lifejacket in the sea of adversity.

You see, leadership, like alchemy, is about transformation, and character is the magical ingredient.

A leader with strong character transforms a group of individuals into a unified, highly functioning team. I've seen it countless times: when trust is earned through honest, open communication, teams go above and beyond.

But character, much like my profession, is something you constantly work at. You can't just rest on your laurels or rely on a title.

Character is about the daily choices you make—choosing what's right over what's easy, honoring commitments, and setting the bar high for yourself.

So, what are my three key ingredients to great leadership of a team or family?

Channeling Bill Hewlett and Dave Packard, it boils down to three things:

- Trust and respect for the individual
- Open and honest communications
- Achieve common objectives through teamwork

Without it, we cannot build successful relationships, families, or communities, and we most certainly cannot successfully build a team without it!

I envision these values stacking like a pyramid, and everything is built upon the foundation of character, which delivers and enables trust and respect for the individual.

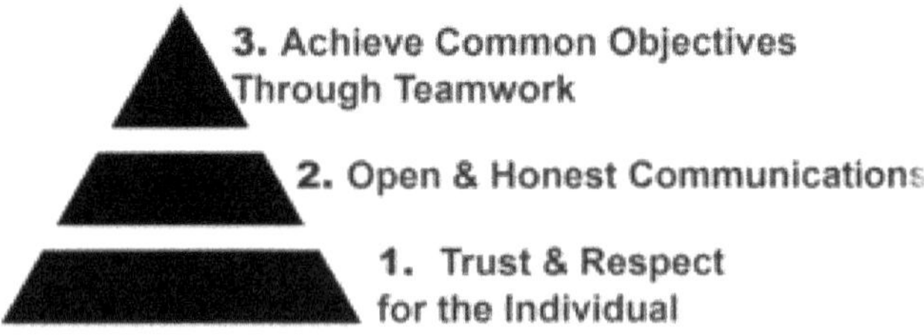

Think of it as the leadership version of *Maslow's Hierarchy of Needs Pyramid*—these are the basic elements that every great leader needs to succeed.

Without character, these principles are as ineffective as trying to power a rocket without fuel. Trust me, it won't get you very far.

Character is more than a trait; it's behavior. It's about keeping promises to yourself, first and foremost.

In the alchemical tapestry of leadership, it's the golden thread that holds everything together. Without it, even the best strategies fail.

I've seen leaders falter when their character wavered, and I've witnessed the triumphs of those who held onto integrity through adversity.

Like the Alchemist, we as leaders are constantly refining ourselves. It's a testament of our own character. It's this relentless pursuit of self-improvement that makes true leadership possible.

When you hold yourself to the highest standards, you not only build strong teams, but you also inspire those around you to be their best.

In the end, achieving your goals without character and integrity is like climbing Mount Everest in flipflops. You might make it to the top, but you'll probably lose a few toes along the way.

So, lace up your boots of integrity, put on your character-filled backpack, and start climbing.

The view from the top is worth it!

Key Points

- **Character is King:** Character is the crucible that defines leadership. Like the integrity of an Alchemist's tools, without it, transformation—whether in teams or individuals—can't happen.

- **Character Runs Deep:** Like an iceberg, most of a person's true character lies beneath the surface and isn't visible at first glance.

- **Life Reveals True Character:** Just as the *Titanic* encountered the hidden strength of an iceberg, our real character shows itself when we face challenges, temptations, or adversity.

- **Integrity is Essential:** Integrity can't be faked or hidden forever; life has a way of revealing who we truly are, especially under pressure.

- **Investing in Integrity:** Building a life of integrity requires time and commitment, but provides a strong foundation that serves us in difficult times.

- **It's Never Too Late to Rebuild:** If trust has been damaged, there's always time to restore it. Integrity is the cornerstone of lasting success in relationships and leadership.

- **Crucial Values of the Leader:** The top three values for a great leader? Trust and respect, open communication, and teamwork. No magic, just integrity and character as the foundation.

- **Character Wins Every Time:** As the great Alchemist, Norman Schwarzkopf, said: "If you must be without one, be without strategy."

Because, at the end of the day, character wins.

CHAPTER 11:
THE ALCHEMY OF VITALITY—THE ENERGY IN LEADERSHIP

The Alchemist harnesses the vital forces for transmutation. Similarly, the Leadership Alchemist infuses vitality, the energetic life force, into leadership, energizing the team and amplifying their collective power of influence.

In the grand tapestry of *The Alchemist's Way*, the fourth principle unfurls as a vibrant thread—*vitality*. It's the lifeblood of leadership, a dynamic force that propels teams toward success.

Vitality isn't just about physical energy; it's the mental and emotional resilience we bring to every challenge, every setback, and every victory.

As Lee Iacocca wisely said, "The speed of the leader is the speed of the team." Without vitality, we risk stalling ourselves and those counting on our momentum.

A leader's vitality radiates outward, setting the tone and pace for the entire team. It empowers us to inspire, persevere, and adapt, even when the path forward is uncertain.

When we're fully energized, even the steepest climbs seem possible, and our energy is contagious.

So why emphasize vitality? Because it's more than physical vigor; it's the enthusiasm and passion we bring to the table that inspires our teams.

We can't expect everyone to show up motivated, and that's where a leader's energy steps in. Vitality fuels not just confidence, but true achievement, growth, and resilience, turning ordinary work into extraordinary accomplishments.

Vitality is sustained through these essentials:

- **Health and Well-Being as the Foundation:** Vitality starts with a healthy body and mind. Leaders who take care of their well-being are more equipped to inspire others without running on fumes. Remember: you can't pour from an empty cup or lead with an empty energy tank!

- **Stepping Beyond the Comfort Zone:** Happiness and progress are often waiting beyond our comfort zones. As the meme states, "Comfort is a drug. Once you get used to it, it becomes addicting. Give a weak person consistent stimulation, tasty food, cheap entertainment, and they'll throw their ambitions right out the window. The comfort zone is where dreams go to die!" Let's not let our dreams gather dust just because the couch is cozy. Whether we step boldly or tiptoe, growth awaits on the other side of the comfort zone.

- **Rest and Renewal:** Sleep is not a luxury—it's vital! Sleep-deprived leaders lack the energy needed to guide and inspire. As Vince Lombardi famously said, "Fatigue makes cowards of us all." So, let's swap exhaustion for vitality, facing each day with the clarity and resilience that only rest can provide.

- **Keeping the Fires Burning:** Stoke those fires of passion! Like any energy source, vitality requires regular refueling. New aspirations, fresh efforts, and even playful challenges keep us energized. It's the secret recipe that keeps us from feeling stale, sustaining the energy we need to lead and achieve.

Nurturing Vitality: A Humorous Twist on Health, Energy, and Purpose

Not every day is a good day, and sometimes our vitality comes with lessons that inspire us not to take our health and vitality for granted. It can vanish in the blink of an eye, and perhaps a recap of this event will best illustrate my point.

Allow me to share my misadventure.

Although weakened from my recovery from pneumonia (first and only bout with pneumonia), I found myself hosting a large family gathering.

All was going well until the laughter and banter of good cheer entered center stage.

In a moment of poor judgment and family bonding, my nephew, a strapping fireman, engaged me in a playful and physical wrestling match. The encounter concluded with a significant lift, followed by a catastrophic fall—yes, right on my back, on the unforgiving tile floor in the great room—a fall that took a mighty toll on the good humor guy and his "fragile" male ego.

Regrettably, I experienced a brief intermission from consciousness and was nonresponsive for a few precious moments.

When I opened my eyes, my nephew, brother, sister, daughter, and dog were leaning over me—talk about a dramatic entrance!

In the months that followed, I learned the hard way that crushing your L1 vertebra comes with a crash course in pain management—and a few quirky new companions. Ibuprofen quickly became my MVP, ice packs were always on standby for overtime, and a rigid body brace turned me into an unintentional expert in awkward mobility.

My days were filled with far too much time spent horizontal and a limping gait that could have earned me a gold medal in the "Slow-Motion Olympics."

For the next three and a half months, I was strapped into a decidedly unflattering full-torso back brace. Picture something that added an extra layer of nerdy charm to my already robust engineering vibe—just with a dash of "mad scientist chic."

In the romance department, let's just say that the body brace was a perfect wingman to an already socially challenged, awkward engineering manager.

On the bright side, I found ways to laugh about it.

Whenever curious kids asked about my brace, I'd tell them I was auditioning for the next Iron Man movie. "Call me Tony Stark," I'd say, trying to sound as heroic as I could from behind the brace.

But underneath the humor, it was tough. My usual vitality? Gone. The spring in my step? Evaporated. Worst of all, my beloved leg day and shoulder workouts were canceled indefinitely. Squats and deadlifts became wistful memories, replaced by "brace adjustment" and the occasional clumsy attempt at mobility practice.

To put it mildly, my spirit groaned as loudly as my joints.

In a fit of self-awareness, I realized that I am no longer the young, fun uncle that I used to be.

Let me tell you, getting old is not for sissies.

When our energy levels are depleted due to injury, poor exercise, or lack of sleep, it wreaks havoc on our day-to-day lives.

Our personal energy is the vitality we bring to our lives, family, and business. It is crucial to our success.

Anthony Robbins said it best, "The higher your energy level, the more efficient your body.

The more efficient your body, the better you feel, and the more you will use your talent to produce outstanding results."

Vitality begins with physiology and establishes the foundation for a growth mindset, so get active daily.

The Leadership Alchemist understands that physical well-being is the cornerstone of vitality. A growth mindset is cultivated on the foundation of a healthy body and mind.

Playing comfortable is not your highest level of service; playing comfortable is not your fullest expression; playing comfortable is not your ultimate end goal, so embrace discomfort and get in shape.

Vitality is the energy source of true attainment, the source of growth, confidence, and the energy we bring to our staff and our projects. It's that secret force that gets us off the couch and pursuing our goals.

In our daily gratitude list, let's make sure to include dedicated thankfulness for our vitality, as it is crucial and ultimately our life source. It is the energy equation that we bring to our teams and one of the core tenets in the Secret Formula for success in leadership, so let's not only acknowledge but nurture this vital force that propels us toward our goals.

Vitality is the fuel we bring to our teams and one of the essential tenets of success in leadership. The Alchemist knows that meaningful goals demand clear, focused, and purposeful energy. With vitality as our driving force, we lead our teams out of the dark comfort zone and into the light of new possibilities.

Like a wellspring, vitality thrives in growth. It encourages us to push boundaries, embrace challenges, and continually evolve. In its absence, stagnation takes root; with vitality, we blossom.

Vitality isn't just an option; it's the secret elixir that propels us from inertia to action, guiding us from our comfort zones toward the achievement of extraordinary goals.

Key Points

- **Vitality is the Fuel for Leadership:** Just as an Alchemist brings life to their craft, a leader brings energy to their team. This isn't just about keeping awake after lunch—it's the enthusiasm that propels the whole team forward. Without it, leading would be like trying to win a car race with flat tires.

- **Health is the Foundation:** Vitality starts with taking care of your physical and mental well-being. When leaders look after themselves, they're better able to inspire others. After all, you can't pour from an empty cup.

- **Get Comfortable Being Uncomfortable:** Progress happens outside the comfort zone. That zone may be cozy, but again, it's also where dreams go to die. So, let's pry ourselves off the couch and stretch a bit—it's amazing what we're capable of outside the comfort barrier.

- **Rest isn't Optional:** Quality rest is essential to vitality. As Vince Lombardi once said, "Fatigue makes cowards of us all." So yes, even heroes need their beauty sleep to stay heroic!

- **Keep the Spark Alive:** Vitality needs regular refueling. Fresh goals and a little adventure keep the energy flowing, ensuring we stay motivated.

Think of it as the secret recipe to prevent leadership from getting stale.

- **Appreciate Vitality While You Have It:** Don't take your vitality for granted, as I learned after a "playful" family wrestling match with my fireman nephew, and months of hobbling, shuffling, limping, and a lot of Ibuprofen later, I now have a renewed appreciation for all things energetic!

CHAPTER 12: THE ALCHEMY OF CONSISTENCY — HABITS THAT SHAPE SUCCESS

In the realm of alchemy, every transformation follows a precise and consistent process. The ancient alchemists knew that without a steady hand and meticulous routine, their experiments would fail, and the transformation of base metals into gold would remain a distant dream. This principle is no different in leadership.

The fifth tenet of *The Alchemist's Way* is all about the alchemy of consistency, and at its core, it's about habits—the daily rituals that, over time, become the pillars of our success.

Why Consistency Matters

Why is consistency so critical to the Alchemist? Because it conquers all excuses.

Consistency keeps you moving forward when obstacles appear, when fatigue sets in, when perfectionism tries to paralyze progress, or when distractions (or the occasional craving for chips and dip) threaten to knock you off course.

Although intensity plays a role in growth, consistency beats intensity every time.

Think of it as a universal law—it's the same principle behind compound interest, strength training, and building strong teams.

- **The Compound Interest Effect:** Just as small, regular investments grow exponentially over time, small, consistent actions in leadership compound, creating powerful results. Each step forward—no matter how small—adds up, creating a momentum that's hard to stop.
- **Strength Training Consistency:** In the gym, the occasional intense workout may leave you sore, but it's the

regular, manageable routines that build lasting strength. The steady push builds resilience, just as consistent, everyday efforts in leadership strengthen our teams and ourselves over time.

- **Team Building with Compounding Impact:** Building strong teams isn't a single grand event; it's the steady practice of showing up, communicating openly, and setting a dependable example. Each small act compounds, creating trust and cohesion that turn a group into a team ready to take on challenges together.

At the core of its success, consistency manifests and enables the full power of the *compound effect*—the steady drumbeat that keeps you on track toward your goals, no matter what challenges arise.

Consistency doesn't just create progress; it transforms small actions into unstoppable forces.

Why is consistency so important to the Alchemist?

Consistency conquers all…

- Consistency conquers obstacles.
- Consistency conquers fatigue.
- Consistency conquers perfection.
- Consistency conquers distractions.
- Consistency conquers betrayal.
- Consistency conquers weariness.
- Consistency conquers depression.
- Consistency conquers weakness.

Consistency wins every time and leads us to the attainment of our goals and freedom.

Imagine your goals as a vast, untamed wilderness. Consistency is the compass that keeps you moving in the right direction. Without it, even the most ambitious plans lose their way.

Like the ancient alchemists who adhered to their precise rituals, the Leadership Alchemist understands the profound impact of daily habits.

Our habits, especially those woven into our morning routines, set the tone for the entire day. They convert the dreamer into the doer and turn aspirations into achievements.

The 90-Minute Pulse of Productivity

Ah, the sacred first burst of daily productivity—my ninety-minute morning ritual is where the day's symphony begins.

Armed with a freshly rested body and a steaming cup of optimism, I dive into this focused sprint.

It's not just productivity; it's setting the day's speedometer, shifting from a peaceful idle to full throttle.

Ninety minutes may seem short, but trust me, with the right mindset, it feels like an alchemist's hourglass turning potential into progress.

By the end, I'm not just ahead of the day; I'm practically leading it by the nose—via caffeinated brilliance in tow.

Warning: Side effects include smug satisfaction and a misplaced belief that I can conquer the world before lunch.

Master the Art of Incrementalism

Small, steady, consistent improvements yield enormous results!

This is the power of incrementalism—a principle so simple yet profound it's like the tortoise and the hare story, but in real life, where slow and steady actually does win the race.

Aristotle knew this centuries ago when he said, *"We are what we repeatedly do. Excellence, then, is not an act, but a habit."* Or as I like to say, "We are what we repeatedly do… so maybe put down the potato chips."

Building great habits is the ultimate act of shaping your future self. Think of each habit as a tiny deposit in the bank of "Future You." Every time you practice a habit, you add value to that account.

To keep this "habit bank" healthy, it's essential to revisit and refine those habits every week. Why weekly? Because habits are like plants—they need regular watering and a little pruning, or they start to wither. Reassessing weekly gives us the chance to catch any "weeds" before they start sprouting in our otherwise perfect garden of habits.

Habits are essential because they turn our big dreams into automatic actions. Once a habit is formed, you don't need motivation to follow through; it's just part of the routine.

Imagine brushing your teeth—easy, right? Now picture brushing your teeth only when you "feel motivated." (Spoiler: that's a pretty bad plan.)

According to University College London, it takes an average of sixty-six days to turn a behavior into an automatic habit. So, patience is key, but also think of it as making yourself a little better every day… with some days better than others.

Every small, intentional step toward your goal compounds over time.

Imagine setting aside just $1 a day for a year—not much at first, but eventually, you've got a nice chunk of change. The same principle applies to our actions: a little effort each day builds up into something big.

It's the difference between finally achieving that fitness goal you've been dreaming about or just investing in a larger, comfier couch.

In the end, habits create our routines— they're the building blocks of our identity. By mastering incrementalism, we shape our outcomes and become the kind of person who can achieve them.

So, let's raise a glass (of water, in the spirit of good habits) to small steps, big wins, and a better you, one routine at a time.

The Ritual of the Morning

Ever wonder what the highest-performing CEOs, Olympic athletes, and top entrepreneurs have in common?

It's not just talent, luck, or a fancy office. It's their non-negotiable morning routines. These habits are their secret sauce, a daily commitment to start the day with intention and purpose.

They hydrate, meditate, reflect, and prioritize. For them, every morning is an opportunity to set the stage for success, much like the Alchemist setting up their workshop for the day's experiments and creation!

In my own journey, my mornings have become my sanctuary—a sacred space where I prepare to face the day.

Picture this: seated in my favorite nook, a high-vantage view of the beautiful Carter Lake in the foothills of the Rocky Mountains. By design, that's how I start my days.

The morning is my moment to get centered before the hustle and bustle of the day begins.

What are my daily habits? A lot like this:

- **Hydrate:** I drink a full glass of water with a generous splash of lemon juice (2+ Tbsp) and a dash of cayenne pepper (more for the truly courageous!).

- **Gratitude and Mindset:** I spend a few minutes in gratitude, reflecting on yesterday's wins and gratitude for today's blessings. It sets the tone for the day, sometimes replaced with guided meditation.

- **Coffee:** Black coffee—my elixir and a morning experience I cherish. (And let's be real, nothing else gets done until that first cup is down.)

- **Direct Energy:** I prioritize top tasks for the day, focus energy where it matters, and commit to three key goals for the day.

- **Productivity Session:** I try to take advantage of the freshly rested body and have a ninety-minute productivity session to set the speedometer tempo for the day—a lot can get done in ninety minutes.

- **Outdoors:** Xander, a rescue lab mix, and I take a forty-plus-minute hike through the foothills of the Rocky Mountains every day.
- **Nourishment:** A protein-rich breakfast to fuel the body and mind.
- **Strength Training:** I strength train almost every day, because, let's face it, at this age, my body has politely informed me (with aches, pains, creaks, and groans) that the weekend warrior days are over. Quite honestly, it's less about conquering the gym and more about staying strong enough to conquer that flight of stairs... and maybe open a stubborn jar of pickles without calling for backup.

The collection of daily habits harmonizes into a constellation that sums up my daily routine (mathematically, it could be rendered as: **Routine = Habit1 + Habit2 + Habit3...).**

These habits are my rituals of daily renewal—a practice that nurtures enthusiasm and primes the spirit for the day's transformative endeavors. Plus, they prevent me from stumbling into work half-awake and hoping nobody notices.

This is not just a routine; it's a ritual. It flexes my consistency muscle and primes my mind for the alchemical feats of the day. And yes, even when life throws a curveball.

Even in my worst moments, these habits were so ingrained that I kept them up in the throes of recovery, and these habits are what keep me grounded and moving forward.

In the end, it's not about grand gestures; it's about showing up every day, consistently, even when you don't feel like it.

Embrace a life of consistent, good daily habits.

Let's be honest—sometimes the toughest feat of the day is getting out of bed and convincing yourself not to press the snooze button for the fifth time.

The Yin and Yang of Habits

Of course, not all habits are created equal. For every brisk hike with my dog Xander, there's the occasional indulgence in pizza or chips and dip. But the magic lies in recognizing the balance, adjusting where needed, and making sure that the positive habits outshine the less productive ones.

Just like the Denver Broncos battling it out on the field, our daily routines are a constant clash of good vs. evil. Our habits determine which side prevails. (And yes, sometimes "Team Chips and Dip" takes the win during a fun Sunday football game.)

Frank Outlaw's Wisdom

"Watch your thoughts; they become words.

Watch your words; they become actions.

Watch your actions; they become habits.

Watch your habits; they become character.

Watch your character; it becomes your destiny."

The Leadership Alchemist understands that the destiny of leadership is intricately woven into the fabric of our habits.

Our morning rituals are the alchemical precision that creates consistency, setting the tone for success. The routine is not just a collection of habits—it's the foundation that supports everything we aspire to achieve.

The Alchemy of Good Habits

Good habits are the unsung heroes of goal attainment. They're the backstage crew in the theater of success, ensuring the spotlight is in the right place, the props are ready, and the curtains open on cue.

So, here's to good daily habits—the silent, consistent drivers of our dreams!

And to those bad habits? Let's laugh, learn, and gently show them the door. (Unless it's chips and dip on game day—some battles are worth losing.)

As we move forward, let's be acutely aware of our habits. Let's reflect on what's working, adjust where necessary, and step into each day ready to be the best version of ourselves.

In the alchemy of leadership, it's the seemingly mundane rituals that create the transformative journey, turning the base metal of routine into the gold of success.

And if you find yourself slipping, don't beat yourself up—just brew a strong cup of coffee, give yourself a pep talk, and get back to it.

Here's to the alchemy of consistency, and to habits that turn our goals into reality.

Key Points

- **Consistency is King:** It conquers obstacles, distractions, fatigue, intensity, and even the occasional late-night snack.

- **Morning Routines Matter:** Top performers across fields have non-negotiable morning habits that set the tone for their success.

- **Habits are the Blueprint:** Good habits form the bedrock of our journey to goal attainment; bad habits are just opportunities for improvement.

- **Daily Reflection and Adjustment:** Be aware of your habits, reflect on their impact, and make necessary adjustments.

- **Routine = Habit1 + Habit2 + Habit3...:** The sum of our habits makes up our daily routine, and our routine determines who we become.

CHAPTER 13: THE ALCHEMY OF THE HEART —THE SERVANT LEADER

The heart of the Alchemist is the true compass, guiding the transformative process. In leadership, it is the servant's heart that defines the Leadership Alchemist—a heart that leads with humility, compassion, and an unwavering focus on others.

A servant leader recognizes that success is never a solo endeavor.

Every achievement is the result of collective effort, where every team member's contributions are valued and celebrated.

With this mindset, the Leadership Alchemist orchestrates success not by commanding, but by empowering, lifting others to their full potential, and creating an environment where growth and collaboration flourish.

In the alchemical tapestry of leadership, the sixth principle gleams with an ethereal radiance—the Heart of the Leader and the Alchemy of Servanthood.

This principle embodies the sacred understanding that leadership, at its core, is a profound privilege intertwined with immense responsibility.

The heart, as the compass guiding the alchemical process, reveals its transformative power in the hands of the leader.

An old sage once said, *"If you don't have the heart to serve, you don't have the heart to lead."*

Leadership is not merely a position; it's a sacred trust—a commitment to the lives entrusted to your care.

The Alchemist understands the enormity of this responsibility, recognizing that the impact of their leadership ripples through the lives of those they touch.

The privilege of leadership is a call to serve, to uplift, and to guide others toward their highest potential.

"Clients do not come first. Employees come first. If you take care of your employees, they will take care of the clients."

—Sir Richard Branson *(Co-founder of the Virgin Group)*

Richard's words are especially true if you are leading others, but the best time to learn it is in your own journey.

For example, when you abandon your New Year's resolutions, lose a game of golf, or fall off your diet, do you beat yourself up, or do you speak kindly to yourself and offer words of encouragement?

The answer to this question is a great indicator as to whether you are ready to step into a leadership role.

Just as we learn to be gentle with ourselves, the Leadership Alchemist learns the art of empathy, compassion, caring, and gentle persuasion.

Mistakes made along the leadership journey serve as poignant lessons.

Lessons from Mother Teresa

Years ago, I met a gentleman.

At first, he struck me as a bit awkward, with a natural inclination toward cynicism. Yet, during our conversation, he shared something that stayed with me.

He claimed to have met and spoken with Mother Teresa of Calcutta.

He went on to tell me that he asked her one question: "With all of the bad in the world, what gives you hope for the future of humanity?"

Her answer, as he relayed it, was both simple and profound.

To paraphrase, she said it came down to two things: *compassion* and *empathy*.

If humanity holds onto these two things, there will always be hope for our future.

I was floored. What an extraordinary response!

As someone born and raised Catholic, her words struck a deep chord within me.

Over time, I found myself reflecting often on her answer, weaving the ideas of compassion and empathy into my own leadership journey. They became more than abstract ideals; they became guiding principles.

So, what does empathy mean to me?

Empathy is the ability to truly see and understand others, to connect with their feelings and perspectives on a deeper level. It's the bridge that allows us to create and sustain meaningful relationships.

And compassion?

Compassion, to me, is empathy in action. It's the driving force that motivates us to help, to give, and to care.

It not only deepens our relationships but also brings a richness and purpose to our own lives. Compassion is what nurtures and cements the most important connections we have.

Mother Teresa's wisdom continues to resonate, shaping not only how I lead but also how I live.

It's a reminder that even in a world filled with challenges, compassion and empathy can light the path forward.

The Heart of the Alchemist

Once again, people don't care about what you know until they learn that you care—caring is the currency of family and teams.

Don't get me wrong. The word "team" translates to work, family, community, and our friends. No one is left behind!

The evolution of leadership is marked by a profound shift in mindset from "me" to "we," understanding that the real strength of a team lies in unity and care for each member.

Reflecting on personal and professional missteps, the realization emerged that leaving individuals behind or fostering an environment where team members feel excluded were the most profound mistakes in my leadership journey.

In the latter years, the focus shifted decisively toward unifying teams and fostering performance cultures rooted in support and care.

The Alchemist, in the pursuit of alchemy with others, understands that true success arises from a collective effort.

The heart of the Alchemist is the compass guiding the intricate process of transformation.

Similarly, the Alchemist, with a servant's heart, orchestrates success not as a solo maestro but as a collaborative symphony conductor.

The acknowledgment that every achievement is a championship ring, and those who practice it get the benefit, underscores the importance of servant leadership.

In the alchemical dance of leadership, the heart becomes the linchpin, uniting diverse talents, temperaments, and ambitions.

As the Alchemist navigates the intricate steps of the transformative journey, it's the beat of the servant's heart that resonates, fostering an environment where each team member contributes harmoniously to the symphony of success.

When it comes to leadership, perhaps The Beatles said it best: "All you need is love."

Key Points

- **It's Not About the Title:** Leadership isn't just about a title; it's a privilege that requires heart and compassion. No heart? No leadership.

- **Leaders Care:** People don't care how much you know until they know how much you care. Seriously, put down the PowerPoint and ask someone how their day is going.

- **Empathy Matters:** Empathy bridges connections by helping leaders deeply understand and relate to others' feelings and perspectives.

- **Compassion Matters:** Compassion, the action-oriented twin of empathy, motivates leaders to help, care for, and build meaningful relationships. Together, these qualities ensure hope and unity, even amidst challenges.

- **The Role of Self-Compassion:** Leaders must first learn to be compassionate with themselves, as this shapes how they treat others and leads to more effective leadership.

- **Lessons from Mother Teresa:** Compassion and empathy are essential for hope in humanity and effective leadership. These principles resonate deeply and serve as guiding lights in fostering meaningful connections.

- **Concoct a Harmonious Jam:** A servant's heart turns leadership into a collaborative symphony, where everyone plays a vital part. Think of it as the world's most harmonious jam session.

- **Love is All You Need:** Sure, love alone won't solve all your problems—but when it comes to leading, it's a pretty good start (and it beats trying to do it all yourself).

CHAPTER 14: WRAPPING UP THE 6 TENETS — MISTAKES? WHAT MISTAKES?

People often ask me, "Why share your mistakes?"

And my answer is simple: every successful journey is paved with missteps and hard-learned lessons.

As mentioned, if I could go back and share a bit of hard-won wisdom with my younger self, I'd do it in a heartbeat.

Since time travel is still not an option (seriously, Elon, what's the hold-up?), I'm sharing these lessons with you instead, hoping that they will light your way forward.

Let's be real—my path was far from perfect. It had more detours and potholes than a backcountry road, even as I delivered over 100 innovations in products and services. The mistakes I've made along the way have kept me grounded, humbled, and hungry to improve.

So, as we recap the six tenets, here are the hard-won lessons behind each one:

- **Mindset:** Early on, discipline was a bit of a stranger to me; the maturity model was a bit elusive. It took time to learn that if I were to lead others, I would first have to lead myself.

- **Goals:** I've botched goals in more ways than I care to admit—setting them poorly, failing to communicate them clearly, or missing opportunities entirely. Over time, I realized that how you set and share your goals matters as much as the goals themselves. That's where the 3 Cs—Compelling, Clear, and Concise—became non-negotiable.

- **Beliefs:** For years, I carried a belief that I couldn't write. It stemmed from school days when teachers suggested I "stick to math and science" and hinted that recess might be my strongest subject. That belief almost became a self-fulfilling prophecy until I decided to challenge it head-on by committing to every difficult path, especially this book. Lesson? Your beliefs, good or bad, shape your actions. Choose them carefully because they can either chain you down or set you free.

- **Character**: When I didn't stay true to myself, broke a promise, ignored performance problems, or didn't call out falsehoods, I should have addressed those challenges head-on. My advice? Keep promises you make to yourself and others. Don't mess this one up. Trust is fragile, and once lost, it's hard to get back. Stay true to yourself and always do the right thing for yourself, your family, and your team.

- **Vitality:** After a serious motorcycle accident, I learned that even achieving goals meant nothing if my health was in tatters. Vitality is that secret sauce that keeps life engaged and meaningful. It is the elixir of leadership, so step out of your comfort zone and work hard!

- **Habit:** Consistency was my game changer. Once I made daily habits a priority (especially my morning routine), my results skyrocketed. It's a key enabler to the compound effect and has changed my life in the most profound ways.

- **Heart:** I've experienced difficult journeys and hollow victories from not serving my teams, family, or groups well. It wasn't until I led with my heart and embraced servant leadership that our achievements and relationships took on true meaning.

The journey to success is never a straight line—it's full of bumps, doubts, and wrong turns. But here's the thing: every mistake, every misstep makes us stronger, sharper, and more resilient.

If you're facing challenges, remember, you're not alone.

Mistakes aren't setbacks; they're proof that you're growing. Mistakes aren't setbacks; they're stepping stones. They show the world that you're trying, learning, and growing.

If there's one thing I hope you take away from this, it's that the journey, mistakes and all, is worth it!

Embrace each lesson, keep moving forward, and maybe, just maybe, we'll both look back on this path and realize it was exactly as it was meant to be—imperfect, yes, but filled with purpose and progress.

And remember, when you do mess up, at least make it a good story.

CHAPTER 15: ALIGNING GOALS TO YOUR PURPOSE

When it comes to finding meaning in our lives, I am 100 percent convinced that each of us was born with a passion for living.

For many, this passion flickers dimly in the corner of life, like an old bulb hanging on for dear life; for others, it burns brightly, illuminating every step of their journey.

Our passion for living awakens as soon as we embrace the very reason for our existence—our *purpose*.

Consider the 3Ps of Aligning Every Facet of Life to Your Purpose

To get the most out of *The Alchemist's Way*, set your goals, align your beliefs, and create habits and routines that align with your purpose, professional and personal aspirations, and you will glean the very most from the lessons shared.

- **Personal:** What lights you up? What experiences bring you joy, satisfaction, and fulfillment? From the people you love to the hobbies you cherish, the personal side of purpose is all about what makes your heart sing (or, in my case, what makes me dance awkwardly but joyfully in the kitchen when no one's watching).

- **Professional:** What goals drive you in your career? What skills do you want to master, and what legacy do you want to leave in your field? Professional purpose isn't just about climbing the ladder; it's about climbing the right ladder—the one that gets you where you truly want to go, without needing a GPS to figure out where you took a wrong turn.

- **Purpose:** The big one. The ultimate "why" behind everything you do. It's the fuel that keeps the engine running, even on the days when you'd rather hit snooze and hide under the covers. Purpose is the anchor that grounds you and the wings that lift you. Without it, you're like a ship drifting aimlessly at sea.

Align Your Goals to That 3P Vision

As the ancient alchemist turned lead to gold, so does today's Alchemist transmute leadership challenges into the golden tapestry of success.

Through the alchemy of clear goals, unwavering belief, impeccable character, vibrant vitality, consistent habits, and a servant's heart, the Leadership Alchemist crafts not just leadership but a legacy—a testament to the enchanting art of *The Alchemist's Way*.

So, what will you do with your one precious, wild, adventurous life?

How will you utilize the sage guidance of the alchemist to attain a better life?

Here's where the fun begins—aligning your goals with your 3P vision. Ask yourself:

- **Who do you want to impact?** The world? Your community? That one friend who still thinks you can't cook because of that one time you burned toast in college?

- **What career goals do you want to check off?** Are you aiming for that promotion, launching your own business, or maybe just getting through your email inbox without breaking into a cold sweat?

- **What countries do you want to visit?** There's a whole world out there waiting to be explored, and your purpose can guide you to new adventures. (Plus, it gives you an excuse to update your passport photo. We all need one.)

- **What business do you want to create?** Maybe it's the next big tech startup, a cozy café, or a revolutionary product that'll change the way people see the world—or just the way they make toast.

- **What dreams are still living in your heart, waiting for new life to be breathed into them?** Dreams don't come with expiration dates. They're like that last piece of cake in the fridge—always there, waiting for you to savor it.

The Alchemist's Way is your tool to help light the path to adventure. It's not just about setting goals; it's about setting the *right* goals—those that align with your passions and lead you to a fulfilling, purpose-driven life.

It's the map to your treasure, and the treasure is becoming all that you were meant to be with a life well-lived.

Key Points

- **The 3Ps Framework:** Align your goals across three core areas—Personal, Professional, and Purpose. When done properly, prepare yourself for a meaningful and beautiful life!

- **Purpose as the Rocket Fuel:** Purpose is the driving force that fuels your passion, keeps you motivated, and guides you toward success and fulfillment extraordinaire!

- **Goal Alignment Is Essential:** To live a purpose-driven life, you must align your personal ambitions, professional aspirations, and life goals with your overarching sense of purpose. You've got this.

- **The Alchemist's Way as a Guide:** Like an alchemist, transform your challenges into successes by using clear goals, belief, vitality, and a servant's heart to craft a legacy and an adventure-filled life!

AUTHOR'S NOTE— THE WHY BEHIND *THE ALCHEMIST'S WAY*

A thirty-seven-year journey, split into two defining events, like mismatched bookends framing a dramatic stage play, handed me not one but two beginnings. This is the story of the *Tale of Two Degrees*—a journey that took me from a fresh-faced engineer, ready to "change the world," to a grizzled single dad with more gray hair than I bargained for and an arsenal of enough dad jokes to rival a comedy tour.

These degrees weren't just milestones; they marked two major life events, exactly thirty-seven years apart, both happening on May 10. The first was in 1987, when I earned my degree in Electrical Engineering. And then, on May 10, 2024, I found myself not earning another degree, but supporting someone far more important—my daughter, Alexa, as she received her degree in Mechanical and Aerospace Engineering.

Back in 1987, I crossed that stage with a head full of formulas, a heart full of ambition, and an abundance of uncertainty. My degree in electrical engineering felt like a passport to the future, a key to unlocking whatever came next. I was ready to power the world, quite literally.

But, as life often reminds us, the equations on paper rarely account for the curveballs that come your way. And believe me, I had my fair share over the years—enough to write a sequel to *The Twilight Zone*. Those curveballs provided lessons that no school could ever teach.

Fast forward to May 10, 2024. It was an even prouder moment than the 37 years prior. My daughter earned her degree, and I was there to cheer her on, knowing that I was passing the torch of engineering to the next generation.

I'll admit it—I was an annoyingly proud single dad that day. Watching her walk across that stage filled me with a sense of joy that no personal accomplishment could match. Her degree was a symbol of continuity, perseverance, and a shared passion for engineering.

Looking back, the only thing more intimidating than my professors in '87 was the prospect of fatherhood. It was something I desperately wanted, but I was terrified of failing. No technical training, no textbook, no blueprint could prepare me for fatherhood.

As Alexa confidently walked across the stage, I realized she had capitalized on her blessings by developing her God-given gifts, leveraging great study habits, and tapping into a deep-felt drive to grow. Unlike her dad, thank goodness she avoided the mullet phase.

Watching her that day, I knew she would surpass anything I ever accomplished. I built the circuits; she's building the future.

When the graduating class ceremoniously shifted their tassels from right to left—the timeless ritual of transition—I held my breath. Not because I was nervous, but because I was witnessing the moment when the torch of engineering officially passed to the next generation (and with bigger ambitions). I mean,

I tackled innovations in computing and consumer electronics; she's setting her sights on mega-rocket propulsion and super space initiatives.

To every single parent out there, I say this: we grew together, and we healed each other. Alexa's journey was my second chance, my opportunity to pass on everything I learned on that long, winding road.

So, what began on May 10, 1987, came full circle on May 10, 2024. These two degrees, separated by exactly thirty-seven years, represent the arc of a journey that wasn't just mine—it's now Alexa's too.

I may have started the story, but she will be the one writing the next chapters. The *Tale of Two Degrees* is about more than personal achievements; it's my call to give back. After leading engineering teams for over thirty-seven years and delivering over 100 innovations, I'm now bequeathing that knowledge to tomorrow's leaders through *The Alchemist's Way*.

Who knows? Maybe thirty-seven years from now, I'll be attending another graduation, watching Alexa's child (my grandchild) receive a degree in "Quantum Gravitational Propulsion Systems" or something equally cool.

Until then, I'll keep engineering the present while she takes charge of the future.

The lessons you'll find in this book are forged from the experiences captured between the bookends of these two degrees. And so, this is where our story begins—a story about legacy, resilience, and the art of turning life's raw materials into gold.

Welcome to *The Alchemist's Way*. Let's begin the transformation.

AFTERWORD—THE LEADERSHIP ALCHEMIST TALE

Once upon a time, in the swirling realm of chaos, there existed a group of lost and frustrated individuals, burdened by fractured team dynamics, ambiguous goals, and poorly defined projects. Misaligned and adrift, they struggled to find their way.

The Leadership Alchemist, a sage warrior with deep scars from hard-fought battles, slowly stepped into the arena.

With a servant's heart and a strategist's mind, the Alchemist began the transformation.

Guided by the compass of clear communication and purpose-driven vision, they charted a course through the stormy seas of confusion. They saw not just tasks and deadlines, but the untapped potential within each individual, waiting to be drawn out.

Under the Alchemist's patient mentorship, the once-misguided individuals began to find their place. Like scattered stars aligning into constellations, the team's orbits shifted toward cohesion.

Nebulous goals, as elusive as shadows, were brought into sharp focus, shaped by the Alchemist's precise strategies and empowering leadership.

Through the crucible of collaboration, where ideas melded like precious metals, the chaotic elements of confusion were refined into a molten stream of cohesive creativity.

The Alchemist, with skillful mastery, orchestrated the symphony of diverse talents, turning the dissonance of discord into a harmonious melody of progress.

In the end, what emerged was nothing short of a masterpiece—a divine *magnum opus*.

The fractured team became a united force, their efforts crystallizing into a beacon of success. The project that once seemed impossible now stood as a shining testament to what could be achieved through vision, resilience, and servant leadership.

The Leadership Alchemist's legacy is now etched in the annals of transformation, a testament to the artistry of turning chaos into creation, and a reminder that even in the most turbulent storms, a skilled guide can lead the way to triumphant victory.

Lead your family, lead your teams, lead your causes, and lead yourself on this journey of life in the footprints of the Leadership Alchemist—*The Alchemist's Way*.

Respect and regards,

The Alchemist, Scarred & Badass Sage of *The Alchemist's Way*

ABOUT THE AUTHOR

Paul Boerger has been leading engineering teams for over 37 years, successfully delivering over 100 innovations in products and services. His career exemplifies a steadfast commitment to excellence, innovation, and the transformative power of leadership.

Drawing from this extensive experience, Paul has developed *The Alchemist's Way*, a proven model of self-mastery and achievement built around six core tenets of leadership.

Designed to inspire and empower aspiring leaders, *The Alchemist's Way* provides practical tools and insights to help you gain more clarity, build unshakable confidence, and expand your influence in the often chaotic and unpredictable world of leadership.

Blending practical wisdom, personal experience, and strategic insight, *The Alchemist's*

Way offers a roadmap for unlocking talents and potential to achieve truly amazing outcomes.

Paul's journey is a powerful testament to his belief that leadership, much like alchemy, is a transformative process—turning raw potential into gold-standard success.

Connect with him at:

- www.thealchemistswaybook.com/
- www.paul-boerger.com/

THE ALCHEMIST'S WAY